Date Due

Centralia			
2 8 1978			
NOV 21 1978			
Sept 25/79			
APR 1 1986			

19628

971.024   Mika, N.
Mik   United Empire
          Loyalists.

2500

2 8 1978	Betty Rook.		
NOV 21	J. Klages		
Sept 25/79	H. Hern		

19628

971.024   Mika, Nick, 1912-
Mik   United Empire Loyalists; pioneers of
          Upper Canada   [By] Nick and Helma Mika.
          Belleville, Ont., Mika, 1976.
              256 p.   illus., maps.
              Includes bibliography.

              1. United Empire loyalists. 2. Canada -
          Hist. - 1763-1791. I. Mika, Helma.
          II. Title.
          0919303099
                                        N-9093
                                        0290009
                                                    6/HE/CN

United Empire Loyalists

United Empire Loyalists

Pioneers of Upper Canada

Nick and Helma Mika

Mika Publishing Company
Belleville, Ont.

1976

UNITED EMPIRE LOYALISTS
PIONEERS OF UPPER CANADA
Copyright © Mika Publishing Company, 1976
ISBN 0-919303-09-9
Printed and bound in Canada
Paper: Baskerville 200M
Type: Melior Light
Printed by The Intelligencer, Belleville, Ontario

Contents

Foreword

In compiling a concise history of the United Empire Loyalists, a fascinating and complex subject, we relied, of course, on material already published — old newspapers, documents, historical papers and records, many books that were written by English, American and Canadian authors. Each writer offers his own interpretation of events. Some, particularly those of earlier days, appear to be prejudiced, and occasionally facts are distorted or, perhaps deliberately, not mentioned at all. Contemporary authors, removed from the emotions of the day, tend to view history far more objectively.

Mrs. Helen Hutchison, historian and curator of the Lennox and Addington County Historical Society's Museum, has supplied us with valuable information, pictures and documents relating to the early Loyalist settlers in the Bay of Quinte area. We sincerely appreciate the contribution she has made to this book.

Much of our research was carried out at the Douglas Library of Queen's University and at the Public Archives of Canada. Many hours were spent at the Belleville Public Library searching for information concerning the Loyalists on the Bay of Quinte.

We are grateful to the officials of the United Empire Loyalists Museum in Adolphustown for allowing us to photograph some of their documents and pictures dealing with the life of the early settlers. We also thank the Hastings County Museum for data, information and valuable pictorial material.

Our special thanks go to the Reverend Bowen B. Squire, Carrying Place, Ontario, for allowing us to use as illustrations some of his pictorial scenes depicting activities of Loyalists in the Bay of Quinte area.

We also wish to express our sincere appreciation to Mr. E. J. Chard of the United Empire Loyalists' Association of Canada for his assistance in locating pictorial material and for lending us the back issues of the *Loyalist Gazette*.

One more explanation. If a great many books have been written on United Empire Loyalists, then why this one? We hope that, with its richly illustrated text, the book will stimulate the interest of young people and entice them to find out more about our Province of Ontario, and how it came to be transformed from a wilderness into a prosperous land where each of us may find happiness and the excitement of discoveries.

We enjoyed researching the history of the United Empire Loyalists, pioneers of Upper Canada who helped to lay the foundation of this province. We hope you will enjoy reading their story.

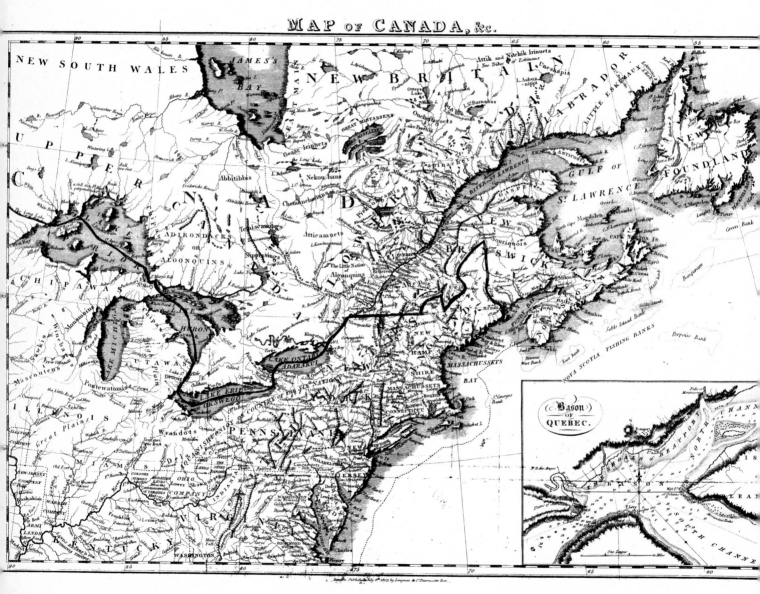

Map of Canada, 1809

Loyalists

The United Empire Loyalists were the offspring of the Revolutionary War between England and her North American colonies. Exiled from the United States of America, they were refugees from an epic conflict that helped to shape the Canadian nation.

The Loyalists left their well-established homes in the American colonies to be scattered in various parts of the globe — some because they were forced to leave, some because they sought adventure, and many because they cherished an ideal.

To understand the motives of these people, who confessed their loyalty to the British Crown in the face of persecution, one must consider their character and their economic circumstances. They were generally peace-loving and law-abiding citizens to whom the thought of revolution was abhorrent. Many, though not all, had prospered under British rule and saw no reason to change their way of life. They felt neither oppressed nor threatened; hence, they did not wish to take part in the American War of Independence.

Loyalists were American colonists like their fellow Americans, the only difference being that they were more complacent in character and felt a deep affection for, if not obligation towards the Crown. This difference in sentiment first emerged shortly after the French and Indian War had ended. It continued to grow, until it separated the colonists into Loyalists and Patriots.

His Majesty George William Frederick the Third, King of Great Britain and Ireland 1760-1820

The Beginning of a
New Era

The long and costly French and Indian War for supremacy in North America ended in 1763. England had gained control of the entire eastern half of the continent. She was at the peak of her power, but her victory harboured serious weaknesses. Her national debt was staggering, amounting to $700,000,000. The vast and complex empire needed to be reorganized. Trade with the colonies demanded policy changes, and the burden of defending her possessions was all but overwhelming.

Congratulatory address to Britain's heroes, King George III, William Pitt, and General Wolfe

King George III was twenty-two years of age when he succeeded to the throne in 1760. His mother had taught him to be a "patriot king", a leader of his people. Aiming to

William Pitt (1708-1778), British statesman. As the head of government during the French and Indian War he directed the operations that led to the British victory in North America.

strengthen the monarchy he demanded that his ministers be responsible to him rather than to Parliament. A minister who disagreed with the King might find himself dismissed and replaced by one less able, but one who managed to please the king.

Grateful to Britain for having removed the threat of French domination in North America, the colonists felt secure and almost absolute masters of their destiny. In congratulatory addresses to the King they pledged their loyalty and gave testimony of their gratitude. Their exultation was a genuine outburst of joy and admiration for the leaders of the British government. In honour of England's prime minister, William Pitt, the colonists renamed Fort Duquesne "Pittsburgh". Massachusetts voted to erect a costly monument in Westminster Abbey, commemorating Lord Howe, who gave his life in the campaign against French Canada.

Map showing location of Fort Duquesne

George Augustus, *Lord Howe*, British general. He was killed leading his men in an attack on Ticonderoga during the French and Indian War, July 6, 1758.

The Fortune Hunters

The first exodus from the thirteen colonies to Canada came shortly after Quebec had been defeated. Those who went to Canada constituted a small group, perhaps less than four hundred. They were mainly merchants, teamsters and sutlers from the New England states and New York who followed the British troops as army contractors and provisioners. Others were land speculators hoping to make fortunes in the conquered land.

The newcomers immediately established contacts with England and organized import and export trade with large business houses in London. The lucrative fur business, which for a century had been the main source of revenue for the French, passed almost overnight into the hands of English traders. It was only natural that the latter should consider themselves part of a privileged class in a country conquered by British and American soldiers.

Accustomed to being governed by representation, Americans in Canada soon objected loudly to the policies of arbitrary power exercised by James Murray, the military Governor of Quebec. Their quarrel with Murray stemmed from his delaying to call promised elections for an Assembly in Quebec, similar to the kind of government back home in Albany, Boston and Philadelphia. Murray knew that in Quebec this would have meant domination by a handful of British over more than eighty thousand French, because at the heart of the matter was the fact that no Roman Catholics were permitted in the elective assembly. Since the French, under the guidance of their parish priests, adhered to their faith despite adversities, they were, of course, excluded from eligibility for election. Under these conditions, Murray refused to have an election.

Pressure mounted. Unable to solve the problems of his occupied territory, Murray left Quebec in 1766, and was replaced by General Guy Carleton.

In the meantime, a new generation was growing. Disbanded British soldiers had stayed in Quebec and married French Canadian girls. Today they are among the Wagners, the Frasers, the McMillans, and the McGregors, old and respected families of Quebec.

James Murray (1722-1794) was appointed military governor of Quebec in 1760. He commanded the British forces in the area during the period of military rule and in 1764 became the first civil governor of the province of Quebec.

View of Montreal, 1760

View of Quebec City

A MAP OF THE
BRITISH EMPIRE,
in NORTH AMERICA.
BY
SAMUEL DUNN, Mathematician.
improved from the Surveys of
CAPT. CARVER.

Map of North America, 1776

The Colonists and English Laws

After the war, the thirteen colonies did not consider themselves one nation. They lived under thirteen individual governments and called themselves not "Americans" but Virginians, Pennsylvanians or New Yorkers. If there were any bond between them, it was the knowledge that they all were British subjects, and they were proud of that.

There was no evidence in 1763 of any desire to change their political system or to declare independence from Britain. Granted, American merchants had grumbled for years about trade restrictions imposed by the mother country, but there were no serious confrontations as yet with Britain concerning the colonists' rights and privileges.

However, England's financial troubles resulted in taxation policies that affected Americans. The mother country expected her colonies to pay their share for the war she had fought on North American soil, and the stage was set for the beginning of a conflict that was so drastically to alter the course of history.

For almost one hundred and fifty years England had left her colonies pretty much to their own devices in internal matters, paying close attention only to trade and commerce. England had looked upon North America as the producer of raw materials and the consumer of British-manufactured goods. Since colonists paid duty on most of their imports, this exchange contributed greatly to the wealth and power of the mother country. To regulate trade with the colonies, a series of laws had been passed between 1660 and 1763, many of them restrictive to the growing ambitions of colonial merchants and traders. Products such as furs, hides, cotton, tobacco and sugar, for example, could only be sold to Great Britain, and none other than British ships were allowed to enter colonial harbours.

Regulations like these were bound to spawn illicit trade, and smuggling had become an accepted way of doing business that proved more than profitable for a great number of Americans. One of Boston's most notorious smugglers was

John Hancock (1737-1793), wealthy colonial merchant and Patriot. He was a member of the Continental Congress from 1775 to 1780, and as the presiding officer in 1776, he was the first to sign the Declaration of Independence.

John Hancock, the man who became the first to sign the Declaration of Independence. Smuggling in the colonies, of course, did not help England's economic woes. British merchants lost sales, and the British government lost revenues.

To stop the growing menace of smuggling, England dispatched warships. Customs officials were authorized to board suspicious ships and search their cargo. On land they were empowered to enter warehouses, shops and private houses in search of illicit goods. In the event of false arrest, the customs official was legally immune. To add insult to injury, lawbreakers were to be tried by an admiralty court. This meant trial without jury. The burden of proof was on the accused. James Otis, a radical Boston lawyer, vigorously protested this practice in court as a violation of Americans' basic right and freedoms. He reminded the court that "a man's home is his castle"; but, he lost his case.

The royal uniform became an unpopular sight, the harsh treatment of merchants was deemed unjust, the court's attitude condemned as tyrannical, and the ill-bred arrogance displayed by some British soldiers did nothing to diminish the hatred building up towards the English establishment.

James Otis (1725-1783), lawyer and American colonial leader. Opposed to the issuance of writs of assistance which enabled royal customs officials to search the establishments of merchants, he appeared as counsel for the merchants of Boston. In his famous address to the court of February 24, 1761, he accused the British government of violating the colonists' basic right and freedoms. His speech gave the Revolutionary movement its slogan: "Taxation without representation is tyranny."

Private of Light Infantry Company, Tenth Regiment of Foot, 1775. (British Army)

The Stamp Act

George Grenville (1712-1770), British statesman. He was leader of the House of Commons and a cabinet member in 1761. In 1762-63 he was first lord of the admiralty and in the following year he was named prime minister, first lord of the treasury, and chancellor of the exchequer. He enacted the Stamp Act which became the chief source of trouble between Great Britain and the American colonies. Grenville was dismissed by George III in 1765.

Unable to curb the well-organized practice of smuggling, England's Chancellor of the Exchequer, Lord Grenville, introduced the Stamp Act in 1765 without realizing that he was stoking the smoldering fires of discontent. The Stamp Act placed a tax on legal documents, newspapers, pamphlets and other printed matter in North America. Pre-stamped paper was to be used, or stamps purchased from government distributors were to be affixed to the item. This was the first direct tax ever levied by England upon the colonists. The revenue from this tax was to support the British army which was on its way to America.

To make things worse, at the request of General Thomas Gage, commanding officer in North America, the "Quartering Act" was introduced which meant that colonists would have to feed and house the British soldiers.

The Acts immediately brought on a storm of protests followed by riots and outbursts of violence. At Williamsburg, Virginia, a country lawyer named Patrick Henry, described as a "rustic and clownish youth of terrible tongue", condemned the proposed Stamp Act as unlawful. He declared that the right of colonists to tax themselves or be taxed by their own representatives was a distinguishing characteristic of the British constitution, and anyone who advised them to comply with the Stamp Act should be declared an enemy of Virginia. The fact was, he pointed out the American colonies were not represented in the British Parliament.

About this time a number of young people secretly organized in Connecticut calling themselves the "Sons of Liberty". The movement quickly spread into Massachusetts, New York, New Jersey and other colonies. Sons of Liberty recognized each other using passwords. Among their leaders were Samuel Adams, John Hancock, Paul Revere, James Otis, and Josiah Quincy. This secret organization gathered information on all colonists suspected of having strong ties with England, and wherever the occasion presented itself, it instigated acts of violence against officials or government sympathizers.

The slogan "No taxation without representation", first shouted by Patrick Henry in Virginia, soon spread throughout the colonies. When the stamps arrived from England most of the colonists refused to buy them. In many instances they were simply snatched by the Sons of Liberty and publicly burned. Organized mobs intimidated and terrorized stamp distributors, dragged them through the streets, vandalized their homes and forced them into resigning their office.

On the Stamp Act issue, colonists received strong support even from members of the British Parliament. "I rejoice," declared William Pitt, "that America has resisted." But the most vociferous advocates for the repeal of the Stamp Act were those British merchants who stood on the brink of bankruptcy because the colonists refused to buy their goods.

In America, the crisis heightened the political differences between the "Tories" who supported the Crown, and the "Whigs" who sided with the rebels. It also created the first political refugees in English America, mostly wealthy people fearing the outbreak of revolution. Among them were Dr. Henry Flower from Pennsylvania, and George Mercer, a stamp collector from Virginia, who left their native land never to see it again.

In May 1766, the British government repealed the controversial Stamp Act. The colonists rejoiced. Church bells rang throughout the land, and special thanksgiving services were held in most churches. Grateful New Yorkers raised money to erect a huge statue of George III, made of gilded lead. Later, when they no longer had any use for the king, they toppled the statue and used the lead to make bullets.

Edmund Burke (1729-1797), British statesman and orator. He studied law, but abandoned it to become a writer. As an opposition member of the British Parliament he sharply criticized George Grenville's policies regarding the American colonies and urged the repeal of the Stamp Act. In his speeches and writings he called for justice and conciliation toward the American colonies.

The announcement of the Stamp Act, which was published in American newspapers, stirred heated debates not only in the American colonies but also in England, where many liberal-thinking statesmen condemned the law. The Stamp Act, passed by the British Parliament in 1765, was designed to raise revenue in the American colonies for the purpose of maintaining British troops in North America.

Sample of stamps to be used on
legal documents.

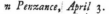
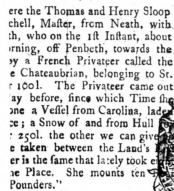

Demonstration against the Stamp Act in New York.

Warning against the use of
stamps.

The publisher of the *Pennsylvania Journal* decided to cease publica-
tion of his newspaper in protest against the Stamp Act.

Stamps being publicly burned on the street.
Incidents like this one took place in many
localities.

When the Stamp Act was repealed on February 22, 1766, all Americans rejoiced, and businessmen on
both sides of the Atlantic breathed sighs of relief. A cartoon in the press depicted the "Funeral of the
Act".

The CRISIS ; *or, a full Defence of the Colonies. In which it is inconteſtibly proved, that the* British Conſtitution *has been flagrantly violated in the late* Stamp Act. (1s. Griffin.)

THE main argument which the enemies of the Colonies make uſe of to juſtify the Act of Parliament in diſpute, is, that the *British* legiſlature has an undoubted right of eſtabliſhing weatever ordinances it may think proper for the regulation of all the *British* dominions ; and that it is an abſolute rebellion againſt the authority of the Mother Country, for any part of thoſe dominions to refuſe an implicit obedience to ſuch ordinances.——To this the *Americans* reply, That, as they are utterly unrepreſented in the Parliament of the Mother Country, a doctrine of this kind muſt inevitably rob them of the moſt valuable rights which they ought to poſſeſs, as *Englishmen,* and reduce them in an inſtant, from a nation of free-born ſubjects, to a ſet of the moſt miſerable ſlaves.——Such is the ſtate of the preſent queſtion.

That the Mother Country has a *power* of impoſing what burdens ſhe thinks proper, on any part of her dominions, is a poſition ſo evident, that it cannot poſſibly admit of a debate. —While ſhe poſſeſſes a *force* capable of exacting an obedience to her laws, ſhe muſt naturally poſſeſs a *power* of enacting whatever may be moſt agreeable to her inclination.—But it does not follow, becauſe ſhe is inveſted with a *power,* that ſhe is inveſted with a *right.*——Nothing can give a *right* which is repugnant to the principles of *equity.*

By the fundamental laws of the *British* conſtitution, it is abſolutely declared, that no *Englishman* is to be taxed without his own conſent.—— Now, if we allow the people of *America* the rights of *Englishmen,* it muſt neceſſarily follow th the Stamp Act is, to the laſt degree, ...equitable ; and that even the conſtitution of the Mother Country itſelf, was flagrantly violated, to lay an arbitrary burden upon the unfortunate Colonies.—— I know very well, I ſhall be told, that tho' the *Americans* are not *immediately* repreſented in the *English* Parliament, they are, nevertheleſs, repreſented *virtually,* and therefore can have no actual foundation for complaint.

If this be the caſe, and this *virtual* repreſentation doth exiſt now, it muſt always have been the caſe, and muſt have exiſted from the beginning.— The Mother Country had as good a right to claim it, from the firſt hour it poſſeſſed a ſingle foot of *ultra marine* territory, as to date her pretenſions entirely from the never to beforgotten period of Mr *Grenville's* adminiſtration.——But why, in the name of common ſenſe, if the Mother Country judged herſelf the *virtual* repreſentative of all her various dependencies, did ſhe grant a provincial legiſlature to her Colonies, and from the time of their firſt exiſtence, inveſt this legiſlature with the ſole power of internal taxation ?—If ſhe meant to grant them a legiſlative power, and yet intended to render this legiſlative power of no conſequence, this would be an equal impeachment both of her juſtice and humanity : It would be an argument, that ſhe abſolutely deſigned to lead the Colonies into an error, for the cruel ſatisfaction of condemning, the moment they unhappily fell into the miſtake.—It would, in ſhort, be an inference, that, for the mere ſake of diſtreſſing *them,* ſhe was reſolved to manifeſt no conſideration whatever for *herſelf.*

Did they not expoſe th lives continually in our ſervice ? a did they not exhauſt their treaſu ſo much beyond the moſt ſangui expectations of the Mother Count that the Parliament of *Great Brit* even voted a very large ſum to rei burſe ſo extraordinary an exertion their munificence ! Poſterity, ſurel muſt be aſtoniſhed to find, at the ve moment we were rewarding the *A ricans* for ſuch inconteſtible proofs their affection, that we were at t ſame time taking away their libertie from a doubt of their fidelity ; th at the very inſtant we expreſſed t greateſt ſenſibility for their attac ment, we puniſhed them with t greateſt cruelty, and accompanied t ſtrongeſt teſtimonies of friendſhip wi the moſt intollerable chains.

The Gentlemen's Magazine and Historical Chronicle, a popular London paper, published an article in 1766 denouncing Britain's policy on the taxation of her colonies.

The Boston Massacre

The Stamp Act was buried, but Britain's new Chancellor of the Exchequer, Charles Townshend, did not want to relinquish Parliament's jurisdiction over the colonies. England needed money and there had to be a way to get it from America. Meanwhile, however, the colonists had developed such a strong resentment to British interference in their affairs, that a clash of arms with the mother country was no longer unthinkable if England did not fully recognize the legislative authority of the colonial governments.

Oblivious to the warning signs, Townshend, like his predecessors, imposed new taxes, this time on lead, glass, paint and tea. Americans reacted swiftly by boycotting all goods imported from England. The British patrol ship, *Gaspee,* aground off Providence, Rhode Island, was attacked and burned. Merchants who bought or sold British goods, found themselves molested on the streets. Their names were published in newspapers, and people were asked not to patronize their shops. Preachers denounced the English government from their pulpits, and local authorities urged Americans to insurrection.

The tension worsened from day to day. The lives of government officials were in danger and streets were unsafe for law-abiding people. When customs officers searched John Hancock's ship, the *Liberty,* for illicit tea and rum, an infuriated mob forced them to flee for their lives. An alarmed Governor Bernard of Massachusetts requested General Gage to dispatch troops from Halifax to Boston to quell the disturbances and protect officials.

Consequently, on September 27, 1768, two regiments under Colonel Dalrymple arrived in Boston harbour where they were greeted with booing and jeering.

Friction between the troops and Bostonians continued to mount. Soldiers found themselves ridiculed and provoked into street brawls. As Samuel Adams put it, they were "the objects of the contempt even of women and children".* The slightest offence a British soldier committed was at once exaggerated out of all proportion.

*W. E. H. Lecky: The American Revolution

In the spring of 1770, on the 5th of March to be exact, there was a scuffle between soldiers and Boston ropemakers. Later that night a gang of civilians roaming the streets taunted a British sentry on King Street. Captain Preston and eight of his men from the main guard post rushed to his aid. With muskets loaded and bayonets fixed, they confronted a dangerous situation. The mob began to shout and stones were thrown. One soldier was struck by a club. Frightened, the others opened fire. Four men lay dead, one was dying. A general uprising that night was averted only when Governor Hutchinson ordered the arrest of Captain Preston and his men.

John Adams and Josiah Quincy, two of the best colonial lawyers and Sons of Liberty at that, defended the accused soldiers in court. All were acquitted except two who were found guilty of manslaughter, branded on the thumb in token punishment, and discharged. But this incident, which went down in history as the "Boston Massacre", was not likely to be forgotten by the Sons of Liberty.

John Adams (1735-1826), second President of the United States. Born in Braintree (now Quincy), Massachusetts. He studied law at Harvard College. In 1764 he married Abigail Smith. John Adams was a leader in the early struggle for American independence.

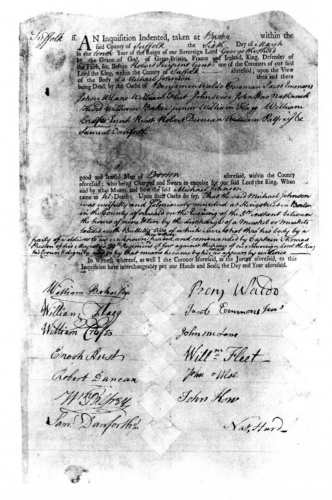

The coroner's inquest into the death of Boston civilians, slain in what became known as the "Boston Massacre".

"The Boston Massacre" as engraved by Paul Revere in 1770, depicting British soldiers shooting down civilians gathered on King Street in Boston on March 5, 1770.

The 29th Regiment have already left us, and the 14th Regiment are following them, so that we expect the Town will soon be clear of all the Troops. The Wisdom and true Policy of his Majesty's Council and Col. Dalrymple the Commander appear in this Measure. Two Regiments in the midst of this populous City; and the Inhabitants justly incensed: Those of the neighbouring Towns actually under Arms upon the first Report of the Massacre, and the Signal only wanting to bring in a few Hours to the Gates of this City many Thousands of our brave Brethren in the Country, deeply affected with our Distresses, and to whom we are greatly obliged on this Occasion—No one knows where this would have ended, and what important Consequences even to the whole British Empire might have followed, which our Moderation & Loyalty upon so trying an Occasion, and our Faith in the Commander's Assurances have happily prevented.

Last Thursday, agreeable to a general Request of the Inhabitants, and by the Consent of Parents and Friends, were carried to their Grave in Succession, the Bodies of *Samuel Gray*, *Samuel Maverick*, *James Caldwell*, and *Crispus Attucks*, the unhappy Victims who fell in the bloody Massacre of the Monday Evening preceeding!

On this Occasion most of the Shops in Town were shut, all the Bells were ordered to toll a solemn Peal, as were also those in the neighboring Towns of Charlestown Roxbury, &c. The Procession began to move between the Hours of 4 and 5 in the Afternoon; two of the unfortunate Sufferers, viz. Mess. *James Caldwell* and *Crispus Attucks*, who were Strangers, borne from Faneuil-Hall, attended by a numerous Train of Persons of all Ranks; and the other two, viz. Mr. *Samuel Gray*, from the House of Mr. Benjamin Gray, (his Brother) on the North-side the Exchange, and Mr. *Maverick*, from the House of his distressed Mother Mrs. *Mary Maverick*, in Union-Street, each followed by their respective Relations and Friends: The several Hearses forming a Junction in King-Street, the Theatre of that inhuman Tragedy! proceeded from thence thro' the Main-Street, lengthened by an immense Concourse of People, so numerous as to be obliged to follow in Ranks of six, and brought up by a long Train of Carriages belonging to the principal Gentry of the Town. The Bodies were deposited in one Vault in the middle Burying-ground: The aggravated Circumstances of their Death, the Distress and Sorrow visible in every Countenance, together with the peculiar Solemnity with which the whole Funeral was conducted, surpass Description.

Description of the funeral of the slain civilians of Boston.

Denunciation of "wicked" monarchs and their ministers.

AMERICANS!
BEAR IN REMEMBRANCE
The HORRID MASSACRE!
Perpetrated in King-street, Boston,
New-England,
On the Evening of March the Fifth, 1770.
When FIVE of your fellow countrymen,
GRAY, MAVERICK, CALDWELL, ATTUCKS,
and CARR,
Lay wallowing in their Gore!
Being *basely*, and most *inhumanly*
MURDERED!
And SIX others badly WOUNDED!
By a Party of the XXIXth Regiment,
Under the command of Capt. Tho. Preston.
REMEMBER!
That Two of the MURDERERS
Were convicted of MANSLAUGHTER!
By a Jury, of whom I shall say
NOTHING,
Branded in the hand!
And *dismissed*,
The others were ACQUITTED,
And their Captain PENSIONED!
Also,
BEAR IN REMEMBRANCE
That on the 22d Day of February, 1770
The infamous
EBENEZER RICHARDSON, Informer,
And tool to Ministerial hirelings,
Most *barbarously*
MURDERED
CHRISTOPHER SEIDER,
An innocent youth!
Of which crime he was found guilty
By his Country
On Friday April 20th, 1770;
But remained *Unsentenced*
On Saturday the 22d Day of February, 1772.
When the GRAND INQUEST
For Suffolk county,
Were informed, at request,
By the Judges of the Superior Court,
That EBENEZER RICHARDSON's *Case*
Then lay before his MAJESTY.
Therefore said *Richardson*
This day, MARCH FIFTH! 1772,
Remains UNHANGED!!!
Let THESE things be told to Posterity!
And handed down
From Generation to Generation,
'Till Time shall be no more!
Forever may AMERICA be preserved,
From weak and wicked monarchs,
Tyrannical Ministers,
Abandoned Governors,
Their Underlings and Hirelings!
And may the
Machinations of artful, *designing* wretches,
Who would ENSLAVE THIS People,
Come to an end,
Let their NAMES and MEMORIES
Be buried in eternal oblivion,
And the PRESS,
For a *SCOURGE* to Tyrannical Rulers,
Remain FREE.

BOSTON, March 12.

THE Town of Boston affords a recent and melancholy Demonstration of the destructive Consequences of quartering Troops among Citizens in a Time of Peace, under a Pretence of supporting the Laws and aiding Civil Authority; every considerate and unprejudic'd Person among us was deeply imprest with the Apprehension of these Consequences when it was known that a Number of Regiments were ordered to this Town under such a Pretext, but in Reality to inforce oppressive Measures; to awe & controul the legislative as well as executive Power of the Province, and to quell a Spirit of Liberty, which however it may have been basely oppos'd and even ridicul'd by some, would do Honor to any Age or Country. A few Persons amongst us had determin'd to use all their Influence to procure so destructive a Measure with a View to their securely enjoying the Profits of an American Revenue, and unhappily both for Britain and this Country they found Means to effect it.

It is to Governor Bernard, the Commissioners, their Confidents and Coadjutors, that we are indebted as the procuring Cause of a military Power in this Capital—The Boston Journal of Occurrences, as printed in Mr. Holt's York Gazette, from Time to Time, afforded many striking Instances of the Distresses brought upon the Inhabitants by this Measure; and since those Journals have been discontinued, our Troubles from that Quarter have been growing upon us: We have known a Party of Soldiers in the face of Day fire off a loaden Musket upon the Inhabitants, others have been prick'd with Bayonets, and even our Magistrates assaulted and put in Danger of their Lives, when Offenders brought before them have been rescued; and why those and other bold and base Criminals have as yet escaped the Punishment due to their Crimes, may be soon Matter of Enquiry by the Representative Body of this People——It is natural to suppose that when the Inhabitants of this Town saw those Laws which had been enacted for their Security, and which they were ambitious of holding up to the Soldiery, eluded, they should more commonly resent for themselves—and accordingly it has so happened; many have been the Squabbles between them and the Soldiery; but it seems their being often worsted by our Youth in those Rencounters, has only serv'd to irritate the former—What passed at Mr. Gray's Rope-walk, has already been given the Public, & may be said to have led the Way to the late Catastrophe—That the Rope-walk Lads when attacked by superior Numbers should defend themselves with so much Spirit and Success in the Club-way, was too mortifying, and perhaps it may hereafter appear, that even some of their Officers were unhappily affected with this Circumstance: Divers Stories were propagated among the Soldiery, that serv'd to agitate their Spirits; particularly on the Sabbath, that one Chambers, a Sergeant, represented as a sober Man, had been missing the preceeding Day, and must therefore have been murdered by the Townsmen; an Officer of Distinction so far credited this Report, that he enter'd Mr. Gray's Rope-walk that Sabbath; and when required of by that Gentleman as soon as he could meet him, the Occasion of his so doing, the Officer reply'd, that it was to look if the Serjeant said to be murdered had not been hid there; this sober Serjeant was found on the Monday unhurt, in a House of Pleasure—The Evidences already collected shew, that many Threatnings had been thrown out by the Soldiery, but we do not pretend to say that there was any preconcerted Plan, when the Evidences are published, the World will judge—We may however venture to declare, that it appears too probable from their Conduct, that some of the Soldiery aimed to draw and provoke the Townsmen into Squabbles, and that they then intended to make Use of other Weapons than Canes, Clubs or Bludgeons.

Our Readers will doubtless expect a circumstantial Account of the tragical Affair on Monday Night last; but we hope they will excuse our being so particular as we should have been, had we not seen that the Town was intending an Enquiry & full Representation thereof.

On the Evening of Monday, being the 5th Current, several Soldiers of the 29th Regiment were seen parading the Streets with their drawn Cutlasses and Bayonets, abusing and wounding Numbers of the Inhabitants.

A few minutes after nine o'clock, four youths, named Edward Archbald, William Merchant, Francis Archbald, and John Leech, jun. came down Cornhill together, and seperating at Doctor Loring's corner, the two former were passing the narrow alley leading to Murray's barrack, in which was a soldier brandishing a broad sword of an uncommon size against the walls, out of which he struck fire plentifully. A person of a mean countenance armed with a large cudgel bore him company. Edward Archbald admonished Mr. Merchant to take care of the sword, on which the soldier turned round and struck Archbald on the arm, then pushed at Merchant and pierced thro' his cloaths inside the arm close to the arm-pit and grazed the skin. Merchant then struck the soldier with a short stick he had, & the other Person ran to the barrack & bro't with him two soldiers, one armed with a pair of tongs the other with a shovel: he with the tongs pursued Archbald back thro' the alley, collar'd and laid him over the head with the tongs. The noise bro't people together, and John Hicks, a young lad, coming up, knock'd the soldier down, but let him get up again; and more lads gathering, drove them back to the barrack, where the boys stood some time as it were to keep them in. In less than a minute 10 or 12 of them came out with drawn cutlasses, clubs and bayonets, and set upon the unarmed boys and young folks, who stood them a little while, but finding the inequality of their equipment dispersed. —On hearing the noise, one Samuel Atwood, came up to see what was the matter, and entering the alley from dock-square, heard the latter part of the combat, and when the boys had dispersed he met the 10 or 12 soldiers aforesaid rushing down the alley towards the square, and asked them if they intended to murder people? They answered Yes, by G—d, root and branch! With that one of them struck Mr. Atwood with a club, which was repeated by another, and being unarmed he turned to go off, and received a wound on the left shoulder which reached the bone and gave him much pain. Retreating a few steps, Mr. Atwood met two officers and said, Gentlemen, what is the matter? They answered, you'll see by and by. Immediately after, those heroes appeared in the square, asking where were the boogers? where were the cowards? But notwithstanding their fierceness to naked men, one of them advanced towards a youth who had a split of a raw stave in his hand, and said damn them here is one of them; but the young man seeing a person near him with a drawn sword and good cane ready to support him, held up his stave in defiance, and they quietly passed by him up the little alley by Mr. Silsby's to Kingstreet, where they attacked single and unarmed persons till they raised much clamor, and then turned down Cornhill street, insulting all they met in like manner, and pursuing some to their very doors. Thirty or forty persons, mostly lads, being by this means gathered in Kingstreet, Capt. Preston, with a party of men with charged bayonets, came from the main guard to the Commissioners house, the soldiers pushing their bayonets, crying, Make way! They took place by the custom-house, and continuing to push to drive the people off, pricked some in several places; on which they were clamorous, and, it is said, threw snow-balls. On this, the Captain commanded them to fire, and more snow-balls coming, he again said, Damn you, Fire, be the consequence what it will! One soldier then fired, and a townsman with a cudgel struck him over the hands with such force that he dropt his firelock; and rushing forward aimed a blow at the Captain's head, which graz'd his hat and fell pretty heavy upon his arm: However, the soldiers continued the fire, successively, till 7 or 8, or as some say 11 guns were discharged.

Article in the *Boston Gazette* describing the "Boston Massacre".

The Boston Tea Party

Although the radicals continued their propaganda, life in the colonies was more stable for the next three years. Businessmen again resumed normal trade with England, and smugglers carried on their activities without much interference. People were tired of meetings, speeches, and violence. Some began to talk of peaceful redress with England and were willing to compromise in order to settle their differences with the mother country. The Tories could point to the fact that England already had retreated twice regarding her policies of taxation and that she was well aware of the colonists' feelings. Then suddenly, in 1773, the British government made a colossal blunder which pushed both sides on a collision course.

The East India Company was faced with bankruptcy. About seventeen million pounds of tea lay unsold in their warehouses. To prevent financial collapse of the company, Parliament granted it a monopoly to sell tea to the Americans at a price far below that of foreign or smuggled tea. This news naturally upset American tea merchants, who had already purchased their supplies at higher prices and now feared financial ruin in the face of this sort of competition sponsored by the King himself.

When the first three ships with tea arrived in Boston harbour in December 1773, Sam Adams and his followers demanded that they return to England without unloading their cargo. Clearance was needed from the Governor, who flatly refused to allow the vessels to depart without the tea duties first being paid by the colonists.

It was the 16th of December, 1773. A well-organized gang of indignant colonists led by the Sons of Liberty, was waiting for a signal at the waterfront. When it was given, some fifty men disguised as Indians, their faces blackened, raced to the wharf and boarded the ships. Sentinels had been posted to keep agents of the authorities at a distance, and for two hours the men unloaded the ships, dumping the cargo of tea into Boston harbour.

England was outraged at the humiliation she had suffered. In retaliation for the daring escapade at Boston, Parliament passed the famous "Intolerable Acts" of 1774.

Boston harbour was to be blockaded by British warships until the tea was paid for. The Charter of Massachusetts was suspended and a new "Quartering Act" was introduced. The right to hold public meetings was suspended also. British officers or soldiers accused of a crime against colonists were not to be tried in the colonies but in England.

Although these Acts were primarily aimed at punishing Massachusetts, all of the American provinces became alarmed. Governor Hutchinson lost his job and was replaced by General Thomas Gage, who arrived with new troops in Boston on the 13th of May, 1774. He was warmly greeted by a group of people who were loyal to England, and who looked upon him as their protector in troublesome times.

On June 1st, the Boston Port Bill went into effect. Patriotic Bostonians printed copies of the Port Bill with a wide black border and posted them on the main streets to be spat upon by passers-by. The news of the closing of Boston's port quickly spread to the other colonies which expressed great concern and sympathy and rushed food and supplies to Massachusetts. The Assembly of Virginia declared the first day of June a day of humiliation, to be spent in fasting and prayer. The colonists then decided to take joint action and representatives from twelve of the colonies were sent to Philadelphia to attend the First Continental Congress.

"The Boston Tea Party". Unwilling to pay duty on imported tea, a group of Boston patriots, disguised as Indians, boarded three British vessels and dumped the ships' cargo of tea into Boston harbour.

On the 15th of July his Excellency is-
fued the following notice:

" Whereas fome foldiers have deferted
his Majefty's fervice, belonging to the
regiments lately arrived from Great Britain and Ireland, this is to give notice,
That all foldiers who deferted from faid
corps previous to the tenth day of this in-
ftant month July, fhall receive their par-
dons, upon furrendering themfelves before or on the tenth day of Auguft next
enfuing; and, on failure of fo doing,
they are not to expect mercy.
    Given, &c.   T. GAGE."

Defertions by British foldiers who sympathized with the American cause, were a
frequent occurrence. They were aided by
the colonists and given civilian clothes.

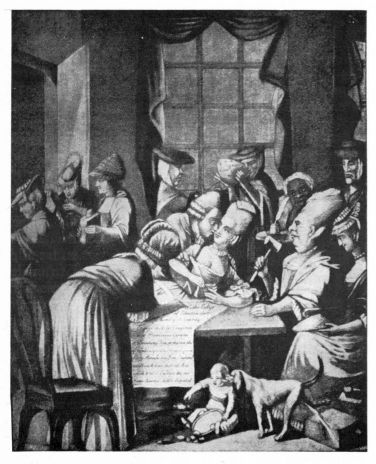

Members of a North Carolina "Society of Patriotic Ladies" pledged
not to drink any tea until England changed her taxation policies.

Bofton, Dec. 20. On Tuefday laft
the body of the people of this and all
the adjacent towns, and others from
the diftance of 20 miles, affembled at
the Old South Meeting-houfe, to en-
quire the reafon of the delay in fend-
ing the fhip Dartmouth, with the Eaft-
India tea, back to London; and having found that the owner had not taken
the neceffary fteps for that purpofe,
they enjoined him at his peril to de-
mand of the Collector of the Cuftoms
a clearance for the fhip, and appointed
a committee of 10 to fee it performed;
after which they adjourned to the
Thurfday following, ten o'clock. They
then met, and being informed by Mr.
Rotch, that clearance was refufed him,
they enjoined him to enter a proteft,
and apply to the Governor for a paff-
port by the caftle, and adjourned again
till three o'clock of the fame day. At
which time they again met, and after
waiting till near fun-fet, Mr. Rotch
came in and informed them, that he
had accordingly entered his proteft, and
waited on the Governor for a pafs, but
his Excellency told him he could not,
confiftent with his duty, grant it until
his veffel was qualified. The people,
finding all their efforts to preferve the
property of the Eaft-India Company,
and return it fafely to London, fruf-
trated by the tea confignees, the Collector of the Cuftoms, and the Governor of the province, diffolved their
meeting.—But, behold what followed!
a number of refolute men (dreffed like
Mohawks or Indians), determined to
do all in their power to fave their
country from the ruin which their enemies had plotted, in lefs than four
hours emptied every cheft of tea on
board the three fhips, commanded by
the Captains Hall, Bruce, and Coffin,
amounting to 342 chefts, into the fea,
without the leaft damage done to the
fhips or any other property. The maf-
ters and owners are well pleafed that
their fhips are thus cleared, and the
people are almoft univerfally congratu-
lating each other on this happy event.

An eye witness description of the events
connected with the "Boston Tea Party".

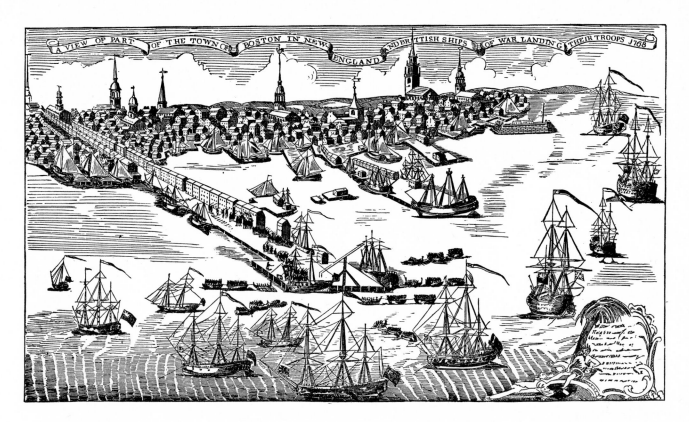

In retaliation for the destruction of tea, Boston harbour was closed and British warships blockaded the entrance.

General Gage, on his arrival at Bofton, on the 13th of May, was received as Governor and Commander in Chief with all poffible honours and refpect. He was complimented on his arrival by his Majefty's Council, by the gentlemen in the commiffion of the peace, by the epifcopal and diffenting clergy, by the military officers, and town magiftrates, and afterwards fumptuoufly entertained at the town-hall.

Next day, there was a numerous meeting of the inhabitants legally affembled at Feneuil-hall, to confider an act of the Britifh parliament for fhutting up their port, when they came to the following refolutions :

"That it is the opinion of this town, *that, if the other colonies come into a joint refolution,* to ftop all importations from, and exportations to, Great Britain, and every part of the Weft Indies, till the act for blocking up this harbour be repealed, the fame will prove the falvation of North America and her liberties.

"That the impolicy, injuftice, inhumanity, and cruelty of the act aforefaid, exceed all our poweis of expreffion. We, therefore, leave it to the juft cenfure of others, and appeal to God and the world."

By thefe refolves, it fhould feem, that a general defpondency has taken place of oppofition, and that they ground their hope of falvation, like a man a-drowning, by catching at the moon.

Bostonians resolve to boycott British importations.

Quebec Act - 1774

Amid angry protests over the treatment of Boston, colonists were shocked to learn of the passage of the Quebec Act which received Royal Assent on May 2, 1774. This act became the basic law, the "Magna Charta", for the French Canadians and ultimately for Canada. The entire northwest territory to the Ohio River, presently occupied by the states of Ohio, Indiana, Illinois, Michigan, Wisconsin, and Minnesota, was annexed to the province of Quebec, thus precluding any westward expansion of New Yorkers, Pennsylvanians and Virginians.

The Quebec Act was a British measure, aimed at smoothing out the difficulties that had arisen from the conquest of New France. It was this bold piece of statesmanship and foresight of Guy Carleton that would keep Canada loyal to England and prevent it from becoming part of the United States. Just how farsighted Carleton was when he implemented the Quebec Act becomes evident more than a hundred years later in the words of Sir E. P. C. Girouard, one of the early graduates of the Royal Military College at Kingston. On June 11, 1915, when he was Assistant to the British Ministry of Munitions, he said at a business meeting in Wales:

> I stand as a British subject and French Canadian. My forefathers resided in Canada for 250 years. We have enjoyed under the British flag the Roman Catholic religion, the French language, the old Napoleonic and pre-Napoleonic law without hindrance and with great tolerance. Is it any wonder the French Canadians feel what it would mean to them and to the Empire as a whole and to the whole world if anything occurred to upset the equilibrium of the Empire?*

The Quebec Act gave French people the right to freedom of worship in the Roman Catholic religion, and permitted them to retain many of their old customs and institutions. Of course, Roman Catholic priests and upper-class French Canadians were greatly pleased. Not so the thirteen colonies. There, the

*Canadian Annual Review, 1915

Quebec Act aroused renewed suspicions of rising French power and encroachment by Papists on the Protestant faith, a threat to their innermost religious sentiments. But most of all, it created resentment, if not outrage, that Americans were prevented from settling the northwestern portion of the continent.

Perhaps if the British Parliament, which granted so many concessions to Canada to please the French Canadian population, had shown as much concern for her thirteen colonies earlier in the conflict, the thought of revolution might never have been born in the minds of Americans.

Catholic priests of Quebec were pleased with the Quebec Act which extended Canada's boundaries to the Ohio River and granted French Canadians free use of their Catholic religion. A cartoon, published in London, England, in July 1774, shows four bishops dancing a minuet around the "Quebec Bill" to music played by British authorities.

THE POLITICAL BOUNDARIES OF QUEBEC

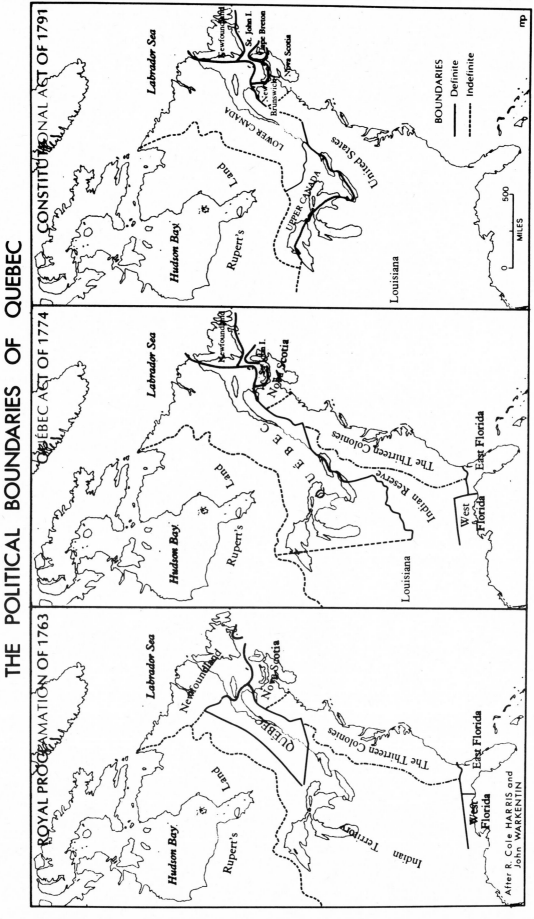

The political boundaries of Quebec in the years 1763, 1774 and 1791.

34

View of Quebec, 1760

Colonists Take A Stand

The time had come when moderately-thinking people in the colonies were beginning to wonder where all the violence, riots and destruction would lead. Although they had never sanctioned them, many had condoned them in the name of "liberty". Fear of a full-blown revolution, however, made them turn to the mother country for protection. They confessed to being "Loyalists", while the radicals described themselves as "Patriots". The die had been cast. The colonists were taking a stand — the Loyalists ready to compromise on issues with the mother country to restore peace, the Patriots poised to fight more determinedly than ever for what they believed to be their rights.

On June 5, 1774, just five days after the closing of Boston harbour, Samuel Adams, together with Joseph Warren and other Sons of Liberty, prepared a document known as the "Solemn League and Covenant", asking colonists to pledge boycott of all commerce with England. Those who refused to sign the document were labelled as "protesters" and marked for harassment. Copies of the "League and Covenant" were dispatched to the other provinces by couriers on horseback.

General Gage at once denounced the League as traitorous, and ordered those who signed the document to be brought to trial. His orders were defied. To his dismay, Gage realized that British authority in the thirteen colonies was on the verge of collapsing. He requested more troops, to keep order and to boost the morale of Loyalists. New barracks were required for the troops, but there was no one in Boston who dared to undertake the construction.

When Gage, on the King's order, replaced a number of judges, magistrates and sheriffs who had been appointed by local governments, there was a vigorous protest. Coerced by Patriots, magistrates in many instances suspended their functions. Those named by Gage to take their place either declined acceptance of the post, or were prevented by mobs from entering their offices. Judges informed Gage that it was impossible for them to function in court as jurors were unwilling to serve for lack of sufficient protection. One judge who had sen-

Samuel Adams (1722-1803), American Revolutionary leader. Born in Boston, Massachusetts, educated at Harvard College. Unsuccessful as a businessman, Samuel Adams turned to politics and became the chief author of the American Revolution. As a literary agitator he fostered the rebellious mood of the colonists. He aroused Bostonians to rebel against the Stamp Act and became the driving force behind the demonstrations challenging the authority of the British Parliament in the American colonies.

tenced a man to prison for forcing his way into the house of a Loyalist in order to confiscate the occupant's rifle, was beaten up and thrown in jail.

Lawyer John Adams, Sam Adams' cousin and like him one of the Sons of Liberty and a Patriot leader, was deeply disturbed by the latest events. He recalled in his diary a conversation he had with a man from Massachusetts:

> "Oh, Mr. Adams, what great things have you and your colleagues done for us. We can never be grateful enough to you. There are no courts of justice now in this province, and I hope there never will be another."

> Is this the object for which I have been contending, said I to myself, for I rode along without an answer to this wretch; are these the sentiments of such people, and how many of them are there in the country? . . . If the power of the country should get into such hands, and there is a great danger that it will, to what purpose have we sacrificed our time, health and everything else?*

Some Patriots, disturbed by the break-down of civil order and the spread of lawlessness, joined the ranks of the Loyalists, prepared to face the consequences. Although claiming to fight for "liberty", the Patriots themselves denied it to those who dared to oppose them. It was perilous to speak out or print anything against the revolutionary movement, as many came to find out. The publisher of one of Philadelphia's leading newspapers received this threat:

> Sir:
> If you print, or suffer to be printed, anything against the rights and liberties of America, or in favour of our inveterate foes, the King, Ministry and Parliament of Great Britain, death, destruction, ruin and perdition shall be your portion.

> Signed by order of the Committee of Tarring and Feathering.

Such was the bitterness of feeling that now animated the Patriots that tarring and feathering became a favourite means of punishing Loyalists who openly dared to defy the Patriots.

On January 25, 1774, one of the coldest days that winter, a Boston mob chose as its target a customs-house official by the name of John Malcolm. He was dragged out of his house and publicly stripped. Hot pine tar was poured over him, which blistered and shrivelled his skin, and while the tar was still soft, he was showered with goose feathers. To add insult to injury, he was hauled around in a cart, spat upon, and ridiculed by the mob. At the Liberty Tree, meeting place of the Sons of Liberty, he was forced to curse the English governor of Massachusetts.

To remove the tar and feathers was a process even more painful than the application. It took hours to peel the hardened tar from the man's body. Skin injuries were unavoidable and infection was almost certain to follow.

* Adams' Works, Vol. II, p. 420

Persecution of a loyay British subject by "tarring and feathering", a favourite means of punishing "Tories", as the rebels called them.

Two Loyalists are victimized by a mob. One man is hoisted high on the liberty pole, and another is waiting his turn to be "tarred and feathered", while the tar is being tested for consistency and a goose is being plucked.

The First
Continental Congress

On September 5, 1774, fifty-six delegates representing twelve colonies (Georgia was not represented) met in Philadelphia at Carpenter's Hall. This was the First Continental Congress. It had assembled to establish the kind of relationship that should be pursued with England after the passing of the "Intolerable Acts", and the closing of the port of Boston.

Quebec and Nova Scotia were not invited for the opening of the session but one month later the Congress sent a message to the "Inhabitants of the Province of Quebec" asking their "affectionate friends and fellow-subjects" to join them in the pursuit of liberty. American and British merchants in Montreal eagerly circulated the request, but without much success. Catholic priests were upset because the Congress had sent a letter to London condemning the "Quebec Act" as supporting a religion "based on bigotry, persecution and murder". Nova Scotia refused to join the Congress because Halifax was established as a naval and military base, and everybody there depended on Britain for their livelihood.

Delegates at the Congress, meanwhile, were divided in their approach to the problems, one group favouring strong measures against England, separation if need be, another group advocating adoption of a moderate course. After heated debates, the "Declaration of Rights and Grievances" was drawn up, denouncing the Intolerable Acts, Admiralty Courts, and taxation as unjust and unconstitutional. An address was forwarded to the King which read in part:

> Your Majesty's Ministers have engaged us in a controversy so peculiarly abhorrent to the affections of your still faithful colonists . . .

Before Congress adjourned on the 20th of October, delegates decided that the resolutions of the "Solemn League and Covenant" of Massachusetts should be adopted by the "Continental Association", thus committing all twelve provinces to the embargo on British goods. Moreover, the creation of a "Committee of Safety" was deemed necessary to guard against elements obstructing the aims of Patriots.

The Patriots at that point in time did not consider England as the greatest danger in the conflict. Their main concern was the Loyalists in their midst, a potential force which had first to be crushed in order to fight the mother country. It had, therefore, been recommended that Patriots everywhere arm themselves and establish in each city, town and county, Committees of Safety and Inspection empowered to apprehend any man-or woman suspected of sympathizing with England, and to interrogate them in a special court of inspection. Such courts were presided over by Sons of Liberty and were reminiscent of the Spanish Inquisition or the secret police of a totalitarian country. Their concern was not so much to pass fair judgement in matters of civil right as to weed out Loyalists and render them inactive in the British cause.

Carpenter's Hall at Philadelphia, meeting place of the First Continental Congress, 1774.

Addrefs to the Inhabitants of Quebec.—

We are too well acquainted with the liberality of fentiment diftinguifhing your nation, to imagine, that difference of religion will prejudice you againft a hearty amity with us. You know, that the tranfcendant nature of freedom elevates thofe who unite in the caufe, above all fuch low-minded infirmities. The Swifs Cantons furnifh a memorable proof of this truth. Their union is compofed of catholic and proteftant ftates, living in the utmoft concord and peace with one another, and thereby enabled, ever fince they bravely vindicated their freedom, to defy and defeat every tyrant that has invaded them.

We do not afk you, by this addrefs, to commence acts of hoftility againft the government of our common fovereign. We only invite you to confult your own glory and welfare, and not to fuffer yourfelves to be inveigled or intimidated by infamous Minifters fo far, as to become the inftruments of their cruelty and defpotifm, but to unite with us in one focial compact, formed on the generous principles of equal liberty, and cemented by fuch an exchange of beneficial and endearing offices as to render it perpetual. In order to complete this highly defirable union, we fubmit it to your confideration, whether it may not be expedient for you to meet together in your feveral towns and diftricts, and elect deputies, who afterwards meeting in a provincial congrefs, may chufe delegates, to reprefent your province in the continental congrefs to be held at Philadelphia, on the tenth day of May, 1775.

In this prefent congrefs it has been with univerfal pleafure, and an unanimous vote, refolved, That we fhould confider the violation of your rights, by the act for altering the government of your province, as a violation of our own; and that you fhould be invited to accede to our confederation, which has no other objects than the perfect fecurity of the natural and civil rights of all the conftituent members, according to their refpective circumftances, and the prefervation of a happy and lafting connection with Great-Britain on the falutary and conftitutional principles herein before mentioned. For effecting thefe purpofes, we have addreffed an humble and loyal petition to his Majefty, praying relief of our grievances ; and have affociated to ftop all importation from Great-Britain and Ireland, after the firft day of December, and all exportations to thofe kingdoms and the Weft-Indies, after the tenth day of next September, unlefs the faid grievances are redreffed.

By order of the Congrefs,
HENRY MIDDELTON, Pref.

Address by the First Continental Congress to the citizens of Quebec urging them to join the American colonies in their pursuit of liberty.

View of the city and port of Philadelphia on the Delaware River.

A LIST of the Names of *those*
who AUDACIOUSLY continue to counteract the UNITED SENTIMENTS of the BODY of Merchants thro'out NORTH-AMERICA; by importing British Goods contrary to the Agreement.

John Bernard,
(In King-Street, almost opposite Vernon's Head.

James McMasters,
(On Treat's Wharf.

Patrick McMasters,
(Opposite the Sign of the Lamb.

John Mein,
(Opposite the White-Horse, and in King-Street.

Nathaniel Rogers,
(Opposite Mr. Henderson Inches Store lower End King-Street.

William Jackson,
At the Brazen Head, Cornhill, near the Town-House.

Theophilus Lillie,
(Near Mr. Pemberton's Meeting-House, North-End.

John Taylor,
(Nearly opposite the Heart and Crown in Cornhill.

Ame & Elizabeth Cummings,
(Opposite the Old Brick Meeting-House, all of Boston.

Israel Williams, Esq; & Son,
(Traders in the Town of Hatfield.

And, **Henry Barnes,**
(Trader in the Town of M   ioro'.

The Sons of Liberty published the names of merchants who refused to boycott the importation of British goods.

Massachusetts Treasury Note, issued in aid of the fight for liberty.

THE good people of the several colonies of New Hampshire, Massachusetts-Bay, Rhode-Island and Providence plantations, Connecticut, New York, New Jersey, Pennsylvania, Newcastle, Kent and Suffex on Delaware, Maryland, Virginia, North Carolina, and South Carolina, alarmed at the arbitrary proceedings of the British parliament and administration, having severally elected deputies to meet and fit in general congress in the city of Philadelphia, and those deputies so chosen being assembled, on the 5th day of September, after settling several necessary preliminaries, proceeded to take into their most serious consideration the best means of attaining the redress of grievances. In the first place, they, as Englishmen, their ancestors, in like cases, had usually done, for asserting and vindicating their rights and liberties, DECLARE,

That the inhabitants of the English colonies in North America, by the immutable laws of nature, the principles of the English constitution, and the several charters or compacts, have the following RIGHTS :—

Resolved, nem. con. 1. That they are entitled to life, liberty, and property; and have never ceded, to any sovereign power whatever, a right to dispose of either without their consent.

Resolved, n. c. 2. That our ancestors were, at the time of their emigration from the mother country, entitled to all the rights, liberties, and immunities, of free and natural born subjects within the realm of England.

Resolved, n. c. 3. That, by such emigration, they neither forfeited, surrendered, nor lost, any of those rights.

Resolved, 4. That the foundation of English liberty, and of all free government, is a right in the people to participate in their legislative council; and, as the English colonists are not represented, and, from their local and

Extracts from the proceedings of the First Continental Congress, 1774, listing the constitutional rights of American colonists as "free and natural born subjects within the realm of England".

43

Early Persecution of Loyalists

Committees for Public Safety began to work at once, supported by local militia. These committees had extraordinary powers, allowing them to arrest and detain people without trial. They could force citizens to appear before them and to answer questions concerning themselves, their friends and neighbours. They could sentence an individual to be publicly flogged, or imprisoned for a specified term and determine the kind of further punishment he was to receive. There were also Committees of Correspondence whose members spread propaganda, kept up communications, and saw to it that any pamphlets written by Loyalists were suppressed or destroyed.

Hundreds of men, friendly to Britain, were apprehended, dragged into the court of public inquiry and forced to sign pledges of support to the Continental Congress and the local government. A few defiant Loyalists who refused to comply with the orders were tarred and feathered and their property was seized. In New Jersey, the estates of no less than five hundred Loyalists were confiscated and sold in small parcels to the militant Patriots.

Similar expropriations occurred in Pennsylvania, Maryland and New York where Delancey's and Roger Morris' lands were divided among five hundred purchasers. Some large holdings of the Anglican church also were confiscated, as was the case in the south.

To escape being insulted, molested and beaten by violent or drunken mobs, Loyalists had two choices: to unite and retaliate with force, or to seek British protection at the nearest garrison. Since the Loyalists for the most part were law-abiding colonists, the thought of resorting to violence was repulsive to them.

When Virginia declared a day of fasting and prayer because of the closing of Boston's port, the Quakers in Pennsylvania were admonished for not observing this day. Their names were published in the paper and they were branded as "Enemies to the Country". The Quakers replied that no cause would receive their support if it contravened their religious principles. Only their church could tell them how to behave and they should be judged accordingly either as foe or friend.

Some of the Loyalists grew tired of hiding. Fear of prosecution caused them to comply with the orders of the Committee of Safety. They renounced their support of the Crown and pledged their devotion to the democratic system.

Punitive measures taken against Loyalists were by no means uniform. They depended largely on the mood and character of the prosecutors, as each committee operated independently. William Davis of Augusta, sentenced for opposing the Sons of Liberty was "drummed" around the Liberty Tree four times and made to apologize publicly for "not knowing what he was doing". Daniel Leonard was compelled to sit on an ice block for ten minutes to "cool his loyalty", while in Virginia, Loyalists were chained to Negros and exhibited in the market square. The Reverend James Nichols of New Cambridge, having been tarred and feathered, was dragged through a muddy brook for hours.

Loyalist, his hands and feet tied, is being brushed with tar while the mob shouts and ridicules him.

If there were any unity, organization or association among the Loyalists at the beginning of the conflict, the Patriots nipped it in the bud; their activities were designed to break up any formation of identity amongst them. The Loyalist leader, Joseph Galloway, familiar with the situation in Pennsylvania, later explained that he had never heard of any association to stand up to the Patriots. Yet, next to New York state, Pennsylvania contained the largest number of Loyalists. General Cornwallis, comparing the two opposing groups, described the Loyalists as "timid" and the Patriots as "aggressive". Thomas Paine, the English writer of *Common Sense* said, "What is Tory? Good God, who is he? I should not be afraid to go with a hundred Whigs against a thousand Tories ... Every Tory is a coward ...".

Loyalists were branded as traitors. They were despised and treated with the utmost contempt. A Loyalist could be charged with high treason for selling food to English soldiers, or refusing to swear allegiance to the revolutionary Committee, or simply for criticizing the Patriots.

To the TORIES.

MIND how ye fight your *Lies* Tomorrow, Gentlemen. As we know ye can't go on without *some*, we'll give ye Leave to use a *few*; but let them be harmlefs ones. A *funny Lie*, or a *merry Lie*, we don't care about; but don't *lie* out of our Reach. None of your *curfed Lies*, that is, none of your Catonian Lies, your Canadian Lies, your religious Lies, nor your commercial Lies; none of your *old Lies* about foreign Troops and Englifh Ambaffadors; none of your *new Lies* about Property and Divifion of Property. In fhort, let's have none of your red-hot ones; none of your two and forty Pounders.---Nothing higher, Gentlemen, than fmall Arms and Swan-fhot; for by Heavens you'll be in a Hobble if you do! And harkee, old Friends, don't put in two for one any more--- remember the Admiralty Juggle.

As I love to fee every Thing go on fair and above board, I have drawn up an Advertifement for ye, which, being a true State of your Cafe, I recommend to you for a Handbill.

To the ELECTORS.

WE, the King's Judges, King's Attornies, and King's Cuftom-Houfe Officers, having had a long Run in this City, grown rich from *nothing at all*, and *engroffed* every Thing to ourfelves, would now moft willingly *keep* every Thing to ourfelves. Wherefore, we earneftly intreat your Support at the State-Houfe Tomorrow, then and there to fecure our Places and Perquifites, by electing fome of us for Burgeffes, in Return for which Favor, we do promife and engage, that when our moft gracious Mafter, the King of Great-Britain, fhall be reinthroned in the Government of thefe provinces, that WE, acting in the Line of our Duty, as *Cuftom-Houfe Officers, Attornies, Judges,* &c. will feize your Property for Smuggling, fue ye for Treafon, condemn ye for Traitors, and hang ye up for Rebels, without charging ye a Farthing.   OLD TRUSTY

Poster against the Loyalists in Philadelphia.

The word "Loyalist" was never used by the rebels. To them they were known only as "Tories". For quick identification, one Philadelphian suggested that all Tories' houses should be painted black. Men like John Adams, however, often protested to the Committee regarding unjust treatment of Loyalists who, according to him, could become useful citizens. When the British army in Boston purchased lumber from a dealer who happened to be a Loyalist, the latter was assaulted by a mob who threatened his life and forced him to renounce his association with the Tories. He went insane and died. Wrote John Adams to his wife:

> The terror and distress, the distraction and horror of his family cannot be described in words or painted upon canvas. It is enough to move a statue to melt a heart of stone to read the story . . .*

Mobs could not be controlled as there was no one who would dare to confront them. British forces were too small in numbers to protect Loyalists living outside the towns and cities. After John Malcolm, the customs collector of Boston, had been brutally tarred and feathered as described earlier, officials living in the country became alarmed at the lack of protection. Henry Hulton, fearing the same treatment as Malcolm, left his property, and moved to Boston. In a letter to a friend, he wrote on February 21, 1775:

> I quitted my habitation in the Country and my family have been with me in Town since the middle of October, as this is the only place of security in the Province for the servants or friends of Government . . .**

Soon treks of Loyalist refugees began to arrive in Boston seeking shelter under the protection of His Majesty's troops. But Boston was already overcrowded, food was scarce, and the situation here was anything but stable. Houses of Loyalists who had been appointed to city council were guarded day and night by soldiers, to prevent a repetition of the tarring and feathering that some of them had suffered earlier.

Sons of Liberty are forcing Loyalists to sign pledges to support the revolutionary cause.

New York, Feb. 10. A body of rioters (calling themselves the Bennington mob) have seized, insulted, and terrified several of the magistrates, and other civil officers, in the northern districts, so that they dare not execute their respective functions ; rescued prisoners for debt ; assumed to themselves military commands and judicial powers ; burned and demolished houses and property, and abused the persons of many of his Majesty's subjects, expelled them from their possessions, put a period to the administration of justice, and spread terror and destruction through that part of the country which is exposed to their oppression. A proclamation has been issued, offering a reward for apprehending the ringleaders.

* Adams' *Familiar Letters*, p. 20
** C. S. Crary: *The Price of Loyalty*

Early Activities of Loyalists

Driven to the point of no return, Loyalists began at last to take some positive steps towards defending themselves.

"If I must be enslaved", said one Loyalist, "let it be by a king at least, and not by lawless committee men. If I must be devoured, let me be devoured by the jaws of a lion and not be gnawed to death by rats and vermin."

The mob activities infuriated most law-abiding citizens. Mather Byles, a member of the Congregational clergy, having seen a tarred and feathered man being dragged through the street, told his neighbour that he "would rather be ruled by one tyrant three thousand miles away, than by three thousand tyrants not a mile away".

On General Gage's suggestion, a body was organized on October 28, 1775, calling itself "The Loyalist Associators desiring the Unity of the Empire". Merchants and traders of Boston raised among themselves two hundred volunteers. General Gage accepted them, and three companies were formed: The Loyal American Associators, the Loyal Irish Volunteers, and the Royal Fencible Americans.

After the Continental Congress had virtually sanctioned the prosecution of Loyalists, resistance to the Committees of Safety began to build up. Governor Tryon of New York declared that if he had the authority, he would burn every committee man's house within his reach. Timothy Ruggles, one of the councillors of Boston, organized a counter committee, a Loyalist Association for the purpose of defending each other's life, liberty, property, and if necessary, enforcing obedience to the king. Another association was formed by Colonel Thomas Gilbert, consisting of three hundred "Loyalists in Massachusetts". In both instances the Committee of Safety soon began to interrogate members of these associations and Patriots marked them for possible intimidation.

The poorly-conducted organization of the Loyalists was blamed on the passive attitude of Gage, who mounted no

Thomas Gage (1721-1787), British general and colonial governor. He was appointed military governor of Montreal in 1761 and was commander of all British forces in North America from 1763 until 1772 when he returned to England. In 1774 he returned again to America, this time as governor and military commander of the Massachusetts colony. In August, 1775, he was appointed commander-in-chief in North America, but resigned two months later and returned once again to England.

effective counter-attack on the Patriots in order to help the suffering Loyalists.

Some Loyalists, rather than having to fight against their neighbours, left the colonies before the first serious clashes occurred. John Coffin took his wife, his eleven children, and all their household goods aboard his schooner *Neptune* and set sail for Quebec. He was bitter, and when the rebels later invaded Canada he volunteered without hesitation as a militiaman to defend his adopted country.

Occasionally, Loyalists managed to escape punishment when defying the rebels' orders. They agreed among themselves beforehand not to sign any pledges, and later at the interrogation each one could argue that none of the others had signed, so why should he?

This kind of sporadic initiative was quickly suppressed by the Patriots, and any confidence the Loyalists might have had in organized resistance of this nature was soon crushed. Moreover, the effectiveness of their efforts to resist was greatly hampered by the lack of rifles, which had been confiscated by the rebels in the early stages of the conflict.

Vernier del   Branche Sc

Early Loyalist exodus to Canada. Two or more families joined to make the journey to new settlements, carrying with them as many of their personal possessions, tools and implements as the wagons would hold.

The Opposing Groups

Patrick Henry (1736-1799), American revolutionary orator, lawyer and statesman. He advocated an open break with the mother country, and as a member of the revolutionary convention of Virginia in 1775, he spoke these famous words: "I know not what course others may take, but as for me, give me liberty or give me death!"

It has been estimated that at the beginning of the American Revolution the population of the thirteen colonies was divided into three groups. One-third stood for change in government, one-third opposed any innovation, and one-third, a neutral group, did not care one way or the other. Naturally, the outcome of the future political system in America depended on the effectiveness of the first two groups in rallying the third group to their cause.

The first segment — the radicals or Patriots as they called themselves — began their activities with an intensive flood of literature supported by English and continental European philosophers. They unified the colonists, at least in their thinking, by pointing to the fundamental right of the individual and the concept of freedom for all men.

The term "Americans" began to surface and gain support among all colonists. The thirteen colonies were economically stable, and prosperity continued to grow. After the successful conclusion of the French and Indian War, Americans no longer felt a need for protection from the mother country, and consequently the relationship between Britain and her colonies changed. The seeds of liberal thinking began to grow into discontent, leading to hostility toward the colonial system.

To guide this liberal group, many dynamic leaders emerged, among them Samuel Adams, Thomas Jefferson, John Adams, Patrick Henry and John Hancock. To lend vigor to the struggle for a new system of government, the "Sons of Liberty" were organized. The "Committee of Correspondence", co-ordinating the activities of colonial agitators, was created. The Continental Congress formed the Committee of Safety, and intimidation of those who disagreed with the revolutionary movement began. Loyalists were disarmed, judges removed from the bench, officials threatened with violence and governors stripped of their authority. Governor Franklin of New Jersey was thrown into jail, Governor Tryon of New York fled to safety, and Governor Martin of North Carolina took refuge on an English warship to escape hanging.

In the meantime the second group, those who opposed radical changes and who called themselves "Loyalists" or "friends of the government", were watching intensely for more than a decade, the spread of discontent, intimidations, and violence without any counter-activities to defend themselves or to stop the growing revolutionary movement. Over the years, the systematic build-up of powerful organizations among the rebels was not challenged in any way by the Loyalists except by timid speeches, writings, and the preachings of some church ministers.

Why did the Loyalists, seeing the danger signals, do nothing to prevent the avalanche?

Well, at the very beginning of the revolution, many Loyalists were in sympathy with the rebels in their fight against the British policy of taxation. But when disorder continued to grow, the Loyalists placed their fate in the hands of the government believing in the strength of the British army. Their spirit of resistance had been supressed by intimidation and the Patriots had seen to it that their weapons had been confiscated in the early stages of the rebellion. Moreover, the Loyalists, later called "United" Empire Loyalists, in the beginning were not united at all, and what was worse, they had no leaders vigorous enough to challenge men like Samuel Adams, Patrick Henry or George Washington.

Loyalists, by and large, acted on an individual basis, bravely, in many instances sacrificing all their possessions, even their lives. The tragedy of their heroism was its futility. Often one unit did not know what another one was doing. Lack of communication and co-ordination eventually led to their downfall.

A New

SONG,

Addreſs'd to the SONS of LIBERTY, on the Continent of AMERICA; particularly to the illuſtrious, Glorious and never to be Forgotten NINETY-TWO of BOSTON.

" The Americans are the Sons, not the Baſtards of England; the Commons of America, repreſented " in their ſeveral Aſſemblies, have ever been in Poſſeſſion of the Exerciſe of this their Conſti- " tutional Right, of GIVING and GRANTING their OWN MONEY; they would have " been SLAVES, if they had not enjoyed it."

Mr. PITT's Speech.

Tune "Come jolly Bacchus" &c. or Glorious firſt of AUGUST."

COME jolly SONS of LIBERTY—
Come ALL with Hearts UNITED,
Our Motto is " WE DARE BE FREE"
Not eaſily affrighted !
Oppreſſion's Band we muſt ſubdue,
Now is the Time, or never ;
Let each Man PROVE this Motto True,
And SLAVERY from him ſever.

See Liberty high poiz'd in Air,
Her FREE BORN SONS commanding,
" Come on, my Sons, without all fear ;
" Your NAT'RAL RIGHTS demanding !
" Your CAUSE, the Gods proclaim, is Juſt,
" Can tamely, you, be fetter'd ?
" In which, diſturb your Fathers DUST !
" With S, be ever letter'd !"

Pale viſſg'd Fear, let none poſſeſs !
Or Terrors e're perplex him,
POSTERITY will ever bleſs,
And nought hereafter vex him ;
To Freedom's Banner, let's Repair ;
When e're we ſee Occaſion—
Nor WIVES nor CHILDREN, tho' moſt dear,
E're ſtop to look, or gaze on.

Obey, my Brothers, Nature's call,
Your Country too demands it !
Let LIBERTY ne'er have a Fall !
'Tis Freedom that commands it.
The Ax, now to the Root is laid,
Will you be, or BOND or FREE ?
No Time to pauſe—then " Whoſe afraid ?"
Live or die in Liberty !

In Freedom's Cauſe, the ſlaviſh Knave,
'Twere better his Condition,
(That might his Country's Ruin ſave !)
To ſink into Perdition ;
Chain'd to a GALLEY, groan his Days,
And never be forgotten,
While Furies croak his Bondage Lays,
After he's Dead and Rotten.

Now FARMER, Dear, we'll fill to you,
May Heav'n its Bleſſings ſhow'r,
As on the Glorious NINETY-TWO,
But Seventeen devour—
Mean abject Wretches !—Slaves in Grain !
How dare ye ſhew your Faces ?
To lateſt Days, go dragg your Chain !
Like other MULES or ASSES.

A SON OF LIBERTY.

Once ſhou'd this PRECEDENT take Place !
Tell, what you call your OWN Sir !
MAGNA CHARTA in Diſgrace !
Your Subſtance now, all flown Sir !
No more ſhall Peers now try your Cauſe !
That Time is now all over !
What need have we pray now of Laws ?
Now Right is Wrong in Trover !

A SONG OF THE REVOLUTION AT THE TIME OF THE MASSA-CHUSETTS CIRCULAR LETTER

A song of the American Revolution refers to the "Glorious Ninety-Two of Boston", who had voted in the Massachusetts Assembly against rescinding the contents of a circular letter sent to the other colonies, and labelled "seditious" by the British government.

Benjamin Franklin's famous cartoon depicting the individual colonies as parts of a disjointed snake, first appeared in 1754 in the *Pennsylvania Gazette*. "Unite or Die" became a slogan of the revolutionary movement.

THE following letter, addressed to Lord NORTH, appears to be of the highest importance. It is therefore printed without abridgment.

My LORD,

AS the arbiter of the affairs of these kingdoms I address your lordship, and cordially hope to engage the impartial attention of your understanding, while I lay before you truths too important to be neglected at this crisis, when the happiness of a brave and loyal people, from wrong apprehensions, is likely to be sacrificed to ministerial power.

The King has not in any of his dominions more affectionate or valuable *people* than the Americans: on every proper occasion they have given undoubted proof of their loyalty, and were actually very valiant during the last war. As father of his country, and head of the legislative body, they honour him; but when he gives his royal assent to laws without due consideration, they never fail to observe and lament it.

Open letter to Lord North, prime minister of Great Britain.

Should your Lordship attempt to enforce, by military discipline, laws they do not acknowledge legal, the consequence will, I fear, be fatal; for so determined are these generous people to preserve inviolate their rights—so justly are they animated by their apprehensions of subjection,—that they would encounter patiently the most terrible difficulties rather than submit; yes, they would

A thorough knowledge of the constitution of this country makes a part of their education; and as they are in general remarkably anxious for the public good, they never forget it. I sincerely wish, my Lord, as much might be said, with truth, of those at home, who have the management of the most important concerns; but it will, I fear, ever be matter of lamentation, that *great men* are so totally debilitated by dissipation, as to render *even* such capacity as heaven has bestowed, useless. That your Lordship may never tremble at the tribunal of the Most High for the abuse of yours, and that England and her colonies may never look back with *horror* to this period, is the unaffected hope of

R.

A woman representing "America" is forced to drink tea by British officials.

First Bloody Confrontation

On April 4, 1775, General Gage received a blacklist from London with orders to apprehend the people named and send them to England for trial. Among the names included were those of Samuel Adams, John Adams and John Hancock. While Gage hesitated, another order arrived ten days later instructing him to take action at once to prevent the rebels from completing their military build-up.

Gage had been told by informers that on April 18, the Committee of Safety was to hold a meeting at Concord and that Adams and Hancock would be there. Under the cloak of strict secrecy, Gage despatched a detachment of elite troops under Lieutenant-Colonel Francis Smith at midnight, with specific orders to seize the rebel leaders and destroy military supplies. Despite elaborate security measures, rebel informers found out about the expedition and notified Paul Revere of the planned attack on Concord. Slipping out of his house, Revere galloped towards Lexington to alert the Patriots.

LORD NORTH.

Frederick North, 2nd Earl of Guilford (1732-1792), British statesman, known as Lord North. As prime minister of Great Britain, he carried out the policies of King George III which led to the American Revolution.

Confrontation at Lexington, Massachusetts.

Meanwhile, Lieutenant-Colonel Smith and 700 of his men had left their barracks. He had been told that a quantity of ammunition, provisions, and a number of cannon and small arms had been collected at Concord for the "avowed purpose of asserting a Rebellion against His Majesty's Government". His orders were to "march with the Corps of Grenadiers and Light Infantry . . . with the utmost expedition and secrecy to Concord where you will seize and destroy all the Artillery and Ammunition, provisions, and all other military store you can find . . ."

The first skirmish of the American Revolution took place at Lexington, Massachusetts, on April 19, 1775. Warned on the preceding night of the approach of the British, about 70 colonial militiamen, known as "minutemen", were waiting for the British soldiers on the village green at Lexington. No one knows who fired the first shot. When the brief encounter was over, eight Americans lay dead and two were wounded. The British marched on to Concord.

BATTLE OF LEXINGTON.

The attempt by the British to seize the rebels' storehouse of arms and ammunition at Concord, Massachusetts, ended in failure. Forced to retreat toward Boston, the soldiers were harassed on the way by a steadily increasing number of colonial militiamen who fired at them from every vantage point.

RETREAT FROM CONCORD.

At daybreak the first British guards reached the village of Lexington, six miles from Concord. Here the British were confronted by about seventy militiamen. The first shot was fired, by whom no one knows. A British officer ordered "fire!". The soldiers fired and advanced with bayonets. When the militia had dispersed, eight Americans lay dead and ten were wounded. After regrouping the British continued to march toward Concord, reaching their destination about 7 a.m.

At Concord, four hundred Americans were waiting on the height above the bridge. The battle began. The British troops withdrew to Boston, leaving behind some seventy dead. Boston was now surrounded by armed and hostile militiamen.

The incidents at Lexington and Concord provoked many colonists into a virtual declaration of independence from Britain. It is said that the first shot fired at Lexington was "heard around the world" as it marked the beginning of the Revolutionary War between England and her colonies, and aroused the spirit of independence far and wide.

Three weeks later, on May 10, 1775, the Second Continental Congress convened at the State House, later Independence Hall, in Philadelphia. About that time, Ethan Allen gathered his troops known as the Green Mountain Boys, at Castleton, Vermont, ready to march towards Lake Champlain and Fort Ticonderoga. During the night the fort was taken by surprise. When the commander of the fort, Captain De la Place, rushed out in his night clothes, he was confronted by Ethan Allen who told him that the fort had been taken by "The Great Jehovah and the Continental Congress." Two days later, the Green Mountain Boys captured the schooner "Liberty" which was to become the first boat of the American navy. But the most important bounty was the capture of fifty-nine artillery guns at the fort, which later in the winter were hauled to Boston to fight the British troops.

Paul Revere (1735-1818), Boston silversmith and engraver. He is famous for his midnight ride on April 18, 1775, when he galloped from Boston to Lexington, warning the settlers of the approach of British troops.

SIEGE OF BOSTON.

Within a few days after the encounters at Lexington and Concord, Boston was besieged by 17,000 rebel troops.

NARRATIVE

OF THE

EXCURSION and RAVAGES,

OF THE

KING's TROOPS, &c.

ON the nineteenth day of April one thousand, seven hundred and seventy five, a day to be remembered by all Americans of the present generation, and which ought and doubtless will be handed down to ages yet unborn, in which the troops of Britain, unprovoked, shed the blood of sundry of the loyal American subjects of the British King in the field of Lexington. Early in the morning of said day, a detachment of the forces under the command of General Gage, stationed at Boston, attacked a small party of the inhabitants of Lexington and some other towns adjacent, the detachment consisting of about nine hundred men commanded by Lieutenant Colonel Smith : The inhabitants of Lexington and the other towns were about one hundred, some with and some without fire arms, who had collected upon information, that the detachment had secretly marched from Boston the preceding night, and landed on Phips's Farm in Cambridge, and were proceeding on their way with a brisk pace towards Concord (as the inhabitants supposed) to take or destroy a quantity of stores deposited there for the use of the colony ; sundry peaceable inhabitants having the same night been taken, held by force, and otherwise abused on the road, by some officers of General Gage's army, which caused a just alarm to the people, and a suspicion that some fatal design was immediately to be put in execution against them : This small

Account of the events at Lexington in the colonial press.

Patriot *Ethan Allen* and his volunteer militia, known as the Green Mountain Boys, captured Fort Ticonderoga in a surprise attack on the morning of May 10, 1775.

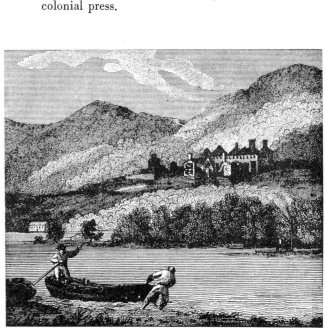

Fort Ticonderoga was built by the French in 1755 on the southern tip of Lake Champlain to guard the approach to Canada. The fort was held in turn by British and by American forces. In 1777 it was recaptured by the British, but was ceded to the United States after the Revolutionary War.

56

Meanwhile, in Philadelphia, John Hancock was elected as president of the Second Continental Congress and George Washington was appointed commander of all American forces. Delegates, acting in a peculiar fashion, resolved on the one hand to send an "Olive Branch Petition" to the King, asking for concessions to and negotiation with his "loyal subjects", while on the other hand they unanimously and quickly agreed to organize an American army.

To the **Kings** *most excellent Majesty*

Most gracious Sovereign,

We your Majesty's faithful Subjects of the colonies of New-Hampshire, Massachusetts bay, Rhode-island and Providence plantations, Connecticut, New-York, New-Jersey, Pennsylvania, the counties of New Castle Kent & Sussex on Delaware, Maryland, Virginia, North-Carolina and South Carolina in behalf of ourselves and the inhabitants of these colonies, who have deputed us to represent them in general Congress, entreat your Majesty's gracious attention to this our humble petition,

The "Olive Branch Petition" sent to the King in the summer of 1775 was one more attempt by the colonists to settle their differences with the mother country by peaceful means. The petition was carried to London by Loyalist Richard Penn, but the King refused to see him.

The State House in Philadelphia, now known as Independence Hall, where the Second Continental Congress convened in 1775.

General George Washington (1732-1799). When he was appointed commander-in-chief of the continental army in 1775, he was faced with the task of turning untrained, undisciplined militiamen into a force capable of fighting the massive British army. In 1789, George Washington became the first President of the United States.

King George III rejected the "olive branch" as a mockery and an insult, and labelled the colonists "rebels". "The die is now cast," said the King, "the colonists must either submit or triumph." England was not anxious to go to war again, especially not against her own colonies inhabited as they were by a great many friends and relatives of the British people. Moreover, the liberal views of some contemporaries in Britain influenced men like General Richard Montgomery, who had served in the British army in the war against the French in America in 1755. When the Revolutionary War started, he refused to serve against the rebels; instead he joined them and fought against the British. The King solved his dilemma by hiring twenty thousand German mercenaries, mostly from the province of Hesse, to assist the British troops.

After the British troops had withdrawn to Boston from Concord, the Patriots besieged the city preventing General Gage from sending out another expedition. Encouraged by the success of their first battle, militiamen seized one British arsenal after another, and rushed supplies of arms towards Boston. Gage and his army were virtual prisoners. Although he was still in command of the city, outside of it his power was reduced to nothing. To break the stalemate, he issued a proclamation offering pardon to all rebels, except Hancock and Adams. The patriots rejected it.

The situation changed when General Howe accompanied by Generals Burgoyne and Clinton, sailed into Boston harbour with a new contingent of British soldiers, on May 25, 1775, bringing the strength of the force in the beleaguered city to ten thousand troops.

On the night of June 16, the Americans occupied an important hill overlooking Boston despite the constant shelling of the position. In the morning, General Howe was sent to dislodge them. Three times the British soldiers attacked, climbing the steep terrain, and were cut down by the murderous fire of the Americans. In the end the British won, but the victory was costly. They had suffered more than one thousand dead and wounded. The American loss was four hundred.

General Gage expressed surprise that the "farmers", as he called the militia, could fight indeed, and fight so fiercely. The Battle of Bunker Hill as it is called, had proved that the British army was not made up of invincible soldiers.

The Battle of Bunker Hill. During the night of June 16, 1775, American forces took possession of Bunker Hill and Breed's Hill, two adjoining heights overlooking Boston harbour, as part of a plan to compel the British to give up Boston. On the morning of June 17 the British, under General William Howe, attacked. Met by heavy fire, they reeled back twice, but a third attack succeeded. It was a costly victory. One thousand one hundred British soldiers had died. The Americans lost four hundred men.

View of Boston from Dorchester Heights. When the American forces occupied Dorchester Heights, General Howe ordered the evacuation of Boston on March 7, 1775.

A Royal Welsh Fusilier of the eighteenth century.

An American Rifle Man in the Revolutionary War.

First Mass Exodus
of Loyalists

Dissatisfied with his performance, the British government recalled General Gage, and in September 1775, General Howe was appointed as the new commander in the American colonies. During the winter of 1775 and 1776, both British and American forces prepared themselves for the next battle. Thanks to the fifty-nine cannon captured at Ticonderoga and dragged by Colonel Henry Knox in a convoy of sleds to the Boston front, General Washington was able to take possession of Dorchester Heights in March 1776. The Continentals at that time had 9,000 troops, which could be reinforced by 5,000 militia if the need arose.

The British were faced with two choices: to attempt to retake the hill and thus remain in control of Boston, or to evacuate the city. Remembering the losses at Bunker Hill, General Howe chose to embark his army and sail to Halifax to await reinforcements from Britain. Evacuation began on March 6, when heavy equipment was loaded aboard ships.

The news of the evacuation struck Loyalists like a death blow. They had sought refuge in Boston and had placed their trust in the British army, secure in their belief that England with its might would soon restore order and punish the rebellious elements. To make things worse, the Loyalists were unable to take all their belongings with them because of restricted accommodation on the few ships available for civilians. Furniture was tossed into Boston harbour. Beautiful hand-made mahogany chests, desks and beds were floating for days in the bay, drifting slowly towards shore.

An eye witness described the tragic departure as a "sad procession of people condemned to death". To some, death would have been preferable. One man by the name of John Taylor committed suicide. When the incident was mentioned to George Washington, his comment was: "It's what a great number ought to have done long ago".

Among the first mass exodus of Loyalists were 102 royal officials, members of government councils, rich landowners, and customs officers. But by far the major portion was

Sir William Howe (1729-1814) succeeded Thomas Gage as commander-in-chief of all British forces in the thirteen colonies. Having evacuated Boston in the spring of 1776, Howe embarked on the New York campaign during which he defeated the Americans on Long Island and took the city of New York. In September, 1777, he occupied Philadelphia, seat of the Continental Congress.

made up of merchants, traders, mechanics and 382 farmers. Wealthy Benjamin Hallowell did not complain when he had to share a small floor space with a few farmers and merchants. There were no berths. Sadness, bitterness, and worry united them as nothing ever had before, helping each other to survive the battle for existence.

One hundred and seventy sailing vessels carried away the English soldiers and 1,100 Loyalist refugees who did not want to remain in Boston at the mercy of the Patriots. Many of these first American Loyalist refugees remained in Nova Scotia. Some went to England, never to see their country again, but they found that personal safety was not sufficient to bring them happiness. These refugees were utterly homesick, so much so that the thought of home haunted them. One Anglican clergyman who had left Boston with many other refugees, could no longer keep silent and revealed his feelings in an article written for a London newspaper: "Every object around me fills me with melancholy . . . I am like a man who has lost all his friends . . ."

As soon as the last vessel had left Boston harbour, Washington and his army triumphantly entered the city.

Boston was evacuated by the British in March, 1776. About 11,000 British soldiers and 1,100 Loyalists sailed for Halifax.

Invasion of Canada

Inspired by the easy conquest of ill-defended Fort Ticonderoga, Ethan Allen with his one hundred and fifty Green Mountain Boys of Vermont, commenced his own war with Canada.

In September, 1775, he crossed the St. Lawrence River hoping to find Montreal full of sympathizers. When he reached the outskirts of the city, he was met by heavily armed British forces. Easily defeated, Allen and his followers were sent to England to be tried as rebels.

About the same time, the Continental Congress, after considerable hesitation while hoping for a peaceful solution to its relations with the mother country, decided to embark officially on war with Canada.

A force of 1,000 volunteers from New York, Connecticut, and New Hampshire, under the command of Richard Montgomery, an English officer who had joined the revolutionists, attacked St. John, Quebec, where Major Preston with seven hundred men, mainly Canadian volunteers from Montreal, put up a brave resistance for more than six weeks.

Another force consisting of 1,100 men, under the command of Benedict Arnold, had started to march from New England toward Quebec City. Arnold took the old route up the Kennebec, across the wilderness portage, to the headwaters of the Chaudière and thence to the St. Lawrence. During this incredible march he lost many men, reaching his destination with only eight hundred men, and these in no condition to fight. After crossing the St. Lawrence, he decided to wait for Montgomery's forces.

Having taken St. John, Montgomery approached Montreal on the 13th of November. Governor Carleton, unable to raise sufficient Canadian volunteers in Montreal despite assistance from Catholic priests, left the city, escaping the enemy with difficulty in a small boat near Sorel. At Quebec City, the last stronghold of British forces in Canada, Carleton prepared for a winter defence.

General Richard Montgomery (1736-1775). Montgomery was born in Ireland. After serving with the British army in America against the French, he settled in New York. At the outbreak of the American Revolution he was appointed brigadier general in the Revolutionary Army. He was killed while leading an unsuccessful assault on Quebec City, on New Year's Eve, 1775.

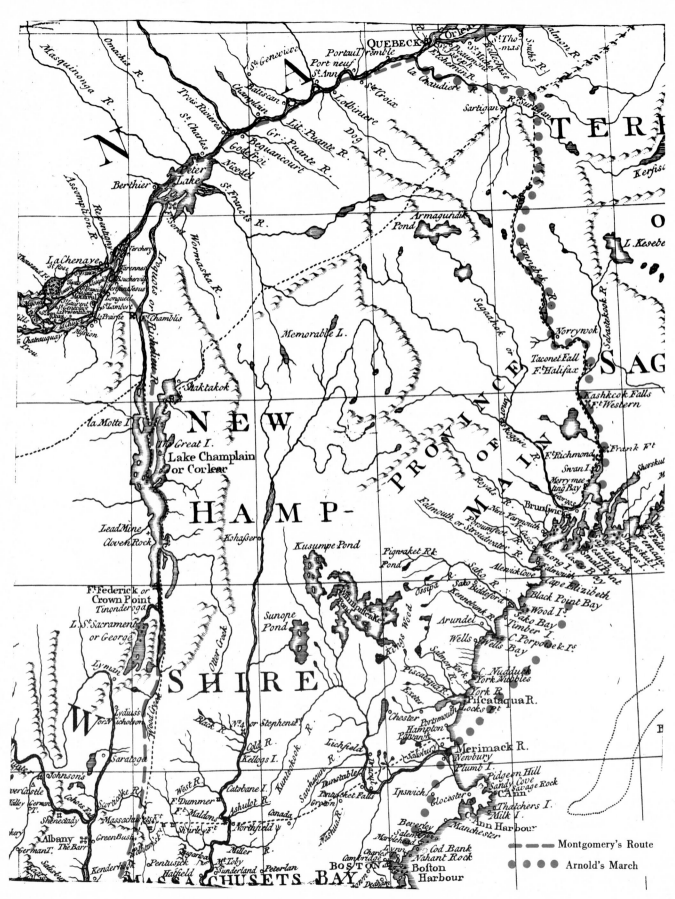

Invasion of Canada, 1775-76. Montgomery's route and Arnold's march.

Governor Carleton reviews his troops on Place D'Armes in Montreal.

On September 25, 1775, Benedict Arnold left Fort Western (now Augusta, Maine) with a force of 1,100 men on the epic march to Quebec. Supplies and men were crammed into clumsy poorly-constructed bateaux that had to be rowed up treacherous rivers, or carried for miles on the shoulders of weary soldiers in order to bypass rapids.

On their march to Quebec through the wilderness of New England, Benedict Arnold's men suffered incredible hardships, struggling against cold, rain and winds of hurricane proportion, their boats damaged and their food spoiled by water. Nearly one third of the force died on the way. Exhausted and near starvation, the rest reached the outskirts of Quebec on November 9, 1775.

In December 1775, Benedict Arnold's army was joined by Montgomery's men from Montreal. Their combined force totalled about two thousand men. While preparing for an assault on Quebec, the American soldiers suffered heavily from the cold of the Canadian winter and an outbreak of smallpox and dysentery. Spirits were low and the men began to talk of going home. Montgomery had no choice but to storm the fortress of Quebec. Early in the morning of December 31, he launched his attack; it ended in disaster: Montgomery was killed and Benedict Arnold wounded. The Americans lost over a hundred dead or wounded and three hundred who were taken prisoner. Disheartened but not defeated, Arnold resumed the blockade of the city with his remaining forces.

Toward the end of April, General Thomas arrived to take command of the Congress troops. A renewed attack on Quebec City was in progress when early in May, 1776, the British fleet sailed up the St. Lawrence with General Burgoyne to rescue the British forces in Quebec. On board the ships were over nine thousand regular troops. General Thomas and his men left Quebec in panic, withdrawing toward Montreal, and then to Lake Champlain.

General Carleton, after reoccupying Montreal, proceeded south taking possession of St. John and the fort at Isle aux Noix and planned to continue his offensive as soon as the necessary supplies and provisions could be obtained.

During Carleton's offensive many Loyalists from Connecticut, Vermont and New York State who had been detained, managed to escape and after weeks of tramping by night and hiding by day, joined the British camp. At Crown Point, Carleton, with some newly formed Loyalist units, attacked the stronghold of the rebels taking prisoners and destroying large quantities of ammunition. It was expected that the British forces would go further south and take Ticonderoga, which was only ten miles from Crown Point. General Carleton, however, knew how much British soldiers loathed the North American winter, and being aware of the Americans' strength at Ticonderoga, he ordered the return to Canada to plan for a spring offensive directed at Albany and New York.

The Loyalists were greatly disappointed. They had left their homes and their families, who were expecting that British soldiers would soon disarm the rebels and return the colonies to their old allegiance.

Sir Guy Carleton

Sir Guy Carleton (1724-1808) was governor of Lower Canada and, until 1777 commander of all British troops in Canada. In 1782 he was appointed commander-in-chief of the British forces in America and had charge of the evacuation of New York. For his services he was created Baron Dorchester and commissioned governor-in-chief of British North America in 1786.

A view of St. Johns (now known as St. Jean, Quebec). During the Revolutionary War St. Johns played a major role as the key to Canada.

Under the cover of a howling snowstorm, General Montgomery attacked the fortress of Quebec on the morning of December 31, 1775.

Benedict Arnold's headquarters near Quebec during the siege of the city in 1775.

General Montgomery was mortally wounded during an unsuccessful assault on Quebec City on New Years Eve, 1775. He had led a column of three hundred men from the Plains of Abraham down a narrow trail to Wolfe's Cove. From there the men had struggled in a blinding snowstorm for two miles along the steep, icy river's edge to Cape Diamond in an attempt to converge on the lower town and link up with Benedict Arnold's men who were approaching from the other side. At Cape Diamond the British had erected a blockhouse, and when Montgomery and some of his men rushed forward, they were showered with cannon and musket fire. Montgomery and two of his officers were instantly killed.

Johnson Hall, Sir William Johnson's residence on the Mohawk River
in Tryon County, New York. Sir William is conferring with the
Indians in front of his house.

THE HIGHLAND COMPANY.
QUEBEC 1835.

True Loyalists

Of all the English colonies in North America, none was more loyal than New York state. Here, on the Mohawk River in Tryon County, Sir William Johnson had built his residence called Johnson Hall. He was superintendent of Indian Affairs for nearly thirty years and wielded a strong influence over the Indians, a factor which at that crucial time helped to sway the majority of them to the Loyalist side. His son, Sir John Johnson, and his sons-in-law Guy Johnson and Daniel Claus, were ardent Loyalists. There were also John and Walter Butler who lived near Caughnawaga, a few miles from Johnstown, and Joseph Brant, Chief of the Mohawk tribe, whose sister, Molly Brant, was the sweetheart of Sir William Johnson.

At the outbreak of the revolution, rebels in New York state tried to persuade the Mohawks and other Six Nations Indians to join them in their fight against supporters of the British Crown. The Mohawks, who lived in villages not far from Fort Hunter, were one of the smallest but perhaps one of the most respected of the Six Nations of the Iroquois Confederacy.

If the Mohawk Valley was a strong pocket of Loyalists thanks to the influence of the Johnsons, there were also firm rebels among the inhabitants. The same was true among the rich and well-known families, many of which were divided in their loyalties. The brother of the rebel General Nicholas Herkimer, Lieutenant-Colonel George Herkimer, was a Loyalist. Another Loyalist Colonel was Henry Frey; his brother Major John Frey, was a rebel and a chairman of the Committee of Safety. The Hooples of Cherry Valley had three sons; two were rebels and the third, Francis, joined the ranks of the Loyalists.

In 1773, on the invitation of Sir William Johnson, a party of over six hundred Scottish Highlanders arrived in New York and settled near Johnstown, the County Town not far from Johnson Hall. The great majority of this party were Catholic emigrants who had come to America to forget their defeat by the English at Culloden, and to find a place where they could live in peace. Instead, they were soon to face a new problem, the American Revolution.

Sir William Johnson Bar.
Major General of the English Forces in North America

Sir William Johnson (1715-1774) was born in Ireland and emigrated to America in 1738, settling in the Mohawk Valley where he acquired a vast estate. Johnson established friendly relations with the Indians, and through his influence the Iroquois sided with the British in the French and Indian War. He was appointed superintendent of Indian Affairs for New York, and was commissioned a major general. For his distinguished services he was created a baronet.

71

Colonel Guy Johnson (1740-1788), Loyalist leader. Born in Ireland, he came to the Mohawk Valley, New York, where he succeeded Sir William Johnson as superintendent of Indian Affairs in 1774. He was well-liked by the Indians and was able to win them to the British side when the conflict between the colonies and the mother country flared into war.

Sir John Johnson (1742-1830), Loyalist leader. He was born in the Mohawk Valley, New York, as the son of Sir William Johnson. In 1774 he inherited his father's estates in the Mohawk Valley, but as a supporter of the Crown, he was forced in 1776 to flee to Canada where he organized and commanded the King's Royal Regiment. His American estates were confiscated, and at the close of the war he settled in Canada.

From the beginning, the Highlanders sided with the Loyalists. In the spring of 1775 Colonel McLean, on instructions from Governor Carleton, raised a corps of volunteers among them, known as the "Royal Highlander Emigrant Regiment".

Colonel Guy Johnson, who had succeeded Sir William Johnson as chief Indian Agent upon the latter's death in 1774, did his utmost to keep the Indian tribes faithful to King George. In the spring of 1775 he received a warning that the Committee of Safety in Albany intended to arrest him and carry him off as prisoner. With a large group of Mohawks, he made his way through the woods to Oswego, where other tribes also declared their intention to support the Crown.

In the meantime, a group of rebels marched into the Mohawk Valley and began to intimidate Loyalists and Indians. Sir John Johnson warned the New York Congress that the Indians would consider it an hostile act, and would attack the white frontier settlements, if any of his people were to be molested or arrested. To pacify the rebels and perhaps to gain more time to organize Loyalists in the Mohawk Valley, he offered to observe neutrality if the New York Congress would leave him and his Highlanders alone.

When the rebels did not reply to his proposition, Sir John began to make preparations for organized resistance. In the summer of 1775, he fortified Johnson Hall and began drilling a militia consisting of 150 men. Early in January, 1776, he sent a message to Governor Tryon in New York: "Having consulted with my friends in this quarter, among whom are many old and good officers, I have come to the resolution of forming a Battalion and have named all the officers . . ."

Somehow this message reached Albany and General Schuyler found it necessary to send a detachment of 3,000 men to disarm Sir John and the Highlanders. Despite the fortifications erected around Johnson Hall, it was impossible to fight against such an overwhelming force. Sir John again gave his parole to Schuyler not to take up arms against the Americans but to remain neutral. As a sign of good faith, the General requested six hostages. Five of them were members of the MacDonald family belonging to the Royal Highlander regiment.

Not to be taken by surprise, Sir John asked friendly Indians to watch for signs of trouble. As expected, trouble was brewing in the spring of 1776. Sir John received a warning from Molly Brant that General Schuyler was sending Colonel Dayton to arrest him, under the pretext that Sir John had broken his promise. The rebels intended to remove him from the Mohawk Valley and secure the Indians to their side. Hastily, Sir John organized a party of 250 followers and with three Indians as guides, dashed toward Canada. Racing against time through forests and across lakes, they reached Montreal, exhausted and destitute.

On June 19, 1776, a regiment was organized, the nucleus of which consisted of the party led by Sir John. It was called the "King's Royal Regiment of New York", also known as "The Royal Yorkers" or more popularly as "Johnson's Royal Greens".

Sir John Johnson's loyalty to the Crown cost him his wealth, his vast holdings, and caused him great personal suffering. His wife was arrested, cast into prison and threatened with hanging. His mansion was plundered, and the tomb of his father, Sir William Johnson, was desecrated. Sir William's leaden casket was melted to make bullets and his remains were scattered.

After the formation of the first corps of Loyalists under Sir John Johnson was completed, two more units were organized. Heading one of these units were the Jessup brothers, Ebenezer, Edward and Joseph, prominent Albany businessmen who had large land holdings along the upper Hudson River. Ebenezer was in command, although it later became apparent that Edward, who was older, was also the more competent, and he took over the leadership. This unit eventually came to be known as "The King's Loyal Americans". The other unit to arrive in Canada around that time was led by John Peters, a native of Connecticut. Most of the men in this group came from the Green Mountains of New Hampshire. Among them was Justus Sherwood, who later became famous as a spy for the British forces. This unit called itself "The Queen's Loyal Rangers".

General Carleton who had returned to Canada, would have preferred to have Jessup's and Peters' groups join him the following spring when he planned his next campaign. Nevertheless, for the time being, he placed them in the charge of Major Gray who in turn was responsible to Sir John Johnson.

By November, 1776, the three Loyalist units had been divided into small groups, and were assigned by British officers as work parties or to distribute provisions. As there was not sufficient barrack space, some of the Loyalists were quartered in French homes at Montreal, or stationed at Vercheres, St. John, Chambly, Lachine, Ste. Anne and Pointe Clair. This was the first winter the men spent separated from their families. As the war continued, many of the relatives they had left behind were subjected to constant harrassment by the rebels, and some families found their way to Canada to join their husbands and fathers.

Joseph Brant (1742-1807), Mohawk Indian Chief and Loyalist. Brant was educated in a Protestant school at Lebanon, Connecticut. He fought on the British side during the Revolutionary War and conducted many daring raids into rebel territory. After the war he led his tribe to the Grand River Valley in Upper Canada, where he was granted a large tract of land. The city of Brantford was named in his honour. Brant's Indian name was Thayendanegea.

THE QUEEN'S OWN (LIGHT INFANTRY) OF
QUEBEC.
1839.

QUEEN'S VOLUNTEERS.

British and French soldie

Street in Albany, N.Y.

North view of Fort Johnson. Sir John Johnson fortified Johnson Hall in the summer of 1775.

Loyalists Begin to Fight

At the time Sir John Johnson and the Highlanders were being disarmed in the Mohawk Valley, Governor Josiah Martin of North Carolina had issued a proclamation calling on all loyal subjects to join him in fighting the rebellious forces.

Among the first to respond to the call was Major Allan MacDonald who, in the autumn of 1775 together with his famous wife Flora, had settled on a large plantation named Killiegray. He was one of hundreds of Highlanders who had come to North Carolina after the disastrous battle at Culloden. When these Highlanders swore the oath of allegiance to the King of England, as they had been obliged to do, they did not take their oath lightly. And when Flora MacDonald decided to support her husband, her influence was felt throughout the Scottish settlement. Her beauty, and the story of her daring rescue of Bonnie Prince Charlie after the Battle of Culloden in 1746, had made her a legendary figure.

Early in February, 1776, she accompanied her husband on a white horse, riding from place to place to persuade fellow clansmen to stand up and defend their homes against the increasing menace of the rebels. She appealed to them to gather at Cross Creek. The clansmen came from far and near. There were the clans of the MacDonalds, MacLeods, MacKenzies, MacRaes, MacLeans, MacLachlans and others. By February 18, fifteen hundred Highlanders and other Loyalists were assembled and ready to march from Cross Creek to Cape Fear. Flora addressed the troops in Gaelic, appealing to their bravery and love of country. The commander of the unit was an old general and hero of Culloden, Donald MacDonald. He was assisted by Colonel Donald MacLeod and Major Allan MacDonald.

According to plans, Governor Martin was to wait for them with one thousand regulars not far from Cross Creek. When the Highlanders arrived and found neither Martin nor his troops there, their spirits sank. They learned that one group of Loyalists, having been intimidated by the rebels earlier, had decided to return home. Governor Martin himself had encountered difficulties too, and had had to seek safety on the

Scottish soldiers of the Highlands.

warship *Cruizer*, barely escaping capture by the rebels. General MacDonald called a council and it was decided to continue toward the coast of Cape Fear, where Sir Henry Clinton was expected to arrive with warships and troops to assist the Loyalists in suppressing the rebels.

In the meantime the rebels, two thousand strong, were waiting at Moore's Creek Bridge blocking the route to the coast. General MacDonald fell ill, and command of the Highlanders was passed to Colonel MacLeod who decided to attack the rebels' stronghold. During the night the rebels lifted the planks from the bridge over Moore's Creek, leaving only greased logs. Unaware of the strength of the rebels, MacLeod advanced bravely at the head of his column. When they reached Moore's Creek they hesitated — there was no bridge! Using two round pine logs to cross, MacLeod, sword in hand, shouted for his men to follow him and dashed towards the enemy. The rebels opened fire.

MacLeod, pierced by twenty balls, fell down. Many were killed or wounded. Over eight hundred Loyalists were taken prisoner. Among those captured was the husband of Flora MacDonald. The Highland Loyalist adventure in North Carolina had ended.

Flora MacDonald (1722-1790), famous Scottish heroine. She helped the pretender to the British throne, Prince Charles Edward, to escape from Scotland after the defeat of his army at Colloden. When it was discovered that she had smuggled the prince, disguised as her maid, to the Isle of Skye, she was imprisoned in the Tower of London. She gained her freedom under the Act of Indemnity, and in 1774 she and her husband, Allan MacDonald, emigrated to North Carolina. Once again she demonstrated what a woman can do, when she mounted her horse on February 18, 1776, and rode up and down the ranks of her clansmen urging them to defend their homes and fight the rebels.

By the KING,

A PROCLAMATION,

For suppressing Rebellion and Sedition.

GEORGE R.

WHEREAS many of Our Subjects in divers Parts of Our Colonies and Plantations in *North America*, misled by dangerous and ill-designing Men, and forgetting the Allegiance which they owe to the Power that has protected and sustained them, after various disorderly Acts committed in Disturbance of the Publick Peace, to the Obstruction of lawful Commerce, and to the Oppression of Our loyal Subjects carrying on the same, have at length proceeded to an open and avowed Rebellion, by arraying themselves in hostile Manner to withstand the Execution of the Law, and traitorously preparing, ordering, and levying War against Us: And whereas there is Reason to apprehend that such Rebellion hath been much promoted and encouraged by the traitorous Correspondence, Counsels, and Comfort of divers wicked and desperate Persons within this Realm: To the End therefore that none of Our Subjects may neglect or violate their Duty through Ignorance thereof, or through any Doubt of the Protection which the Law will afford to their Loyalty and Zeal; We have thought fit, by and with the Advice of Our Privy Council, to issue this Our Royal Proclamation, hereby declaring that not only all Our Officers Civil and Military are obliged to exert their utmost Endeavours to suppress such Rebellion, and to bring the Traitors to Justice; but that all Our Subjects of this Realm and the Dominions thereunto belonging are bound by Law to be aiding and assisting in the Suppression of such Rebellion, and to disclose and make known all traitorous Conspiracies and Attempts against Us, Our Crown and Dignity; And We do accordingly strictly charge and command all Our Officers as well Civil as Military, and all other Our obedient and loyal Subjects, to use their utmost Endeavours to withstand and suppress such Rebellion, and to disclose and make known all Treasons and traitorous Conspiracies which they shall know to be against Us, Our Crown and Dignity; and for that Purpose, that they transmit to One of Our Principal Secretaries of State, or other proper Officer, due and full Information of all Persons who shall be found carrying on Correspondence with, or in any Manner or Degree aiding or abetting the Persons now in open Arms and Rebellion against Our Government within any of Our Colonies and Plantations in *North America*, in order to bring to condign Punishment the Authors, Perpetrators, and Abettors of such traitorous Designs.

Given at Our Court at St. *James's*, the Twenty-third Day of *August*, One thousand seven hundred and seventy-five, in the Fifteenth Year of Our Reign.

God save the King.

LONDON:
Printed by *Charles Eyre* and *William Strahan*, Printers to the King's most Excellent Majesty. 1775.

A PROCLAMATION BY KING GEORGE III., AUGUST, 1775.

Reproduced from one of the original broadsides in Dr. Emmet's collection now in the Lenox Library.

Movement Toward Independence

In January, 1776, a pamphlet written by Thomas Paine and entitled *Common Sense*, was published urging colonists to commit themselves to independence. Paine's writings inspired people as nothing ever had before. In less than three months 120,000 copies were sold and read by everyone who sympathized with the American cause. The final page of *Common Sense* carried a single line advocating "The Free and Independent States of America".

On April 12, 1776, North Carolina became the first province to empower its delegates to the Second Congress at Philadelphia to join others who might advocate independence from Britain. Virginia, however, was the first to take action. On June 7, 1776, Richard Henry Lee of Virginia moved that "these united Colonies are and of right ought to be free and independent States, that they are absolved from all allegiance to the British Crown...". John Adams of Massachusetts seconded the motion.

On June 11, 1776, a committee, consisting of Thomas Jefferson, Benjamin Franklin, John Adams, Roger Sherman, and Robert Livingston, was appointed to prepare a declaration of independence in accordance with Lee's resolution. Thomas Jefferson, a 33-year-old lawyer from Virginia with a reputation for his literary skill, wrote the document. After lengthy debates and several minor changes made by the committee and by Congress, the final draft of the *Declaration of Independence* was adopted on July 4, 1776, by a unanimous vote of the delegates of twelve colonies. The representatives of New York did not vote because they had not been authorized to do so. However, on July 9, 1776, the New York Provincial Congress endorsed the Declaration of Independence.

Two months prior to the signing of the Declaration, the delegates in Philadelphia had been deeply divided on the issue of independence. Some believed that independence was forced upon an unwilling people and that it was perilous to separate

Thomas Jefferson,

Thomas Jefferson (1743-1826), a Virginia lawyer, was one of the most prominent intellectuals of his day. In 1774 he presented a set of resolutions to the Virginia convention, dealing with the rights of the colonists and repudiating the authority of the British Parliament over the American colonies. As a member of the Continental Congress, he drafted the Declaration of Independence in 1776. In 1800 he became the third President of the United States.

from Britain; others warned that it was advocated prematurely. In the end most of the opponents signed the document.

John Adams, who had led the fight for the adoption of the declaration in Congress, wrote to his wife Abigail: ". . . it (July 4th) ought to be celebrated, as the day of deliverance, by solemn acts of devotion to God Almighty. It ought to be solemnized with pomp and parade, with shows, games, sports, guns, bells, bonfires and illuminations, from one end of this continent to the other, from this time forward, evermore."

First draft of the Declaration of Independence.

Benjamin Franklin (1706-1790). Franklin was almost 70 years old when the Revolution began. As a printer, author, philanthropist, inventor, scientist, statesman and diplomat, he was known on both sides of the Atlantic.

He was born in Boston where he attended school for a short time and began to work in his father's tallow shop. With one dollar in his pocket, he reached Philadelphia in 1723 and started to work at the *Pennsylvania Gazette*. Soon he became a part owner, and at the age of 24, the sole owner of the newspaper. His famous *Poor Richard's Almanack* made its first appearance in 1732 and was edited by him until 1757.

In 1776 Franklin was sent to Canada to persuade Canadians to join the North American colonies in their struggle for independence. He took an active part in the Second Continental Congress and the drafting of the Declaration of Independence.

In CONGRESS, JULY 4, 1776.

A DECLARATION

BY THE

REPRESENTATIVES

OF THE

UNITED STATES

OF

AMERICA,

IN GENERAL CONGRESS ASSEMBLED.

WHEN in the course of human events, it becomes neceffary for one people to diffolve the political bands which have connected them with another, and to affume among the powers of the earth, the feparate and equal ftation to which the laws of nature and of nature's God entitle them, a decent refpect to the opinions of mankind requires that they fhould declare the caufes which impel them to the feparation.

We hold thefe truths to be felf-evident, that all men are created equal, that they are endowed by their Creator with certain unalienable rights, that among thefe are Life, Liberty and the Purfuit of Happinefs.——That to fecure thefe Rights, Governments are inftituted among men, deriving their juft powers from the confent of the Governed, that whenever any form of Government becomes deftructive of thefe ends, it is the right of the people to alter or to abolifh it, and to inftitute new Government, laying its foundation on fuch principles, and organizing its powers in fuch form, as to them fhall feem moft likely to effect their fafety and happinefs. Prudence, indeed will dictate that Governments long eftablifhed fhould not be changed for light and tranfient caufes; and accordingly all experience hath fhewn, that mankind are more difpofed to fuffer, while evils are fufferable, than to right themfelves by abolifhing the forms to which they are accuftomed. But when a long train of abufes and ufurpations, purfuing invariably the fame object, evinces a defign to reduce them under abfolute defpotifm, it is their right, it is their duty, to throw off fuch Government, and to provide new guards for their future fecurity. Such has been the patient fufferance of thefe Colonies; and fuch is now the neceffity which conftrains them to alter their former fyftem of Government. The hiftory of the prefent King of Great-Britain, is a hiftory of repeated injuries and ufurpations, all having in direct object the eftablifhment of an abfolute Tyranny over thefe ftates. To prove this, let facts be fubmitted to a candid world.

He has refufed his affent to laws, the moft wholefome and neceffary for the public good.

He has forbidden his Governors to pafs laws of immediate and preffing importance, unlefs fufpended in their operation till his affent fhould be obtained; and when fo fufpended, he has utterly neglected to attend to them.

He has refufed to pafs other laws for the accommodation of large diftricts of people, unlefs thofe people would relinquifh the right of reprefentation in the legiflature, a right ineftimable to them, and formidable to tyrants only.

He has called together legiflative bodies at places unufual, uncomfortable, and diftant from the depofitory of their public records, for the fole purpofe of fatiguing them into compliance with his meafures.

He has diffolved reprefentative Houfes repeatedly, for oppofing with manly firmnefs his invafions on the rights of the people.

He has refufed for a long time, after fuch diffolutions, to caufe others to be elected; whereby the legiflative powers, incapable of annihilation, have returned to the people at large for their exercife; the ftate remaining in the mean time expofed to all the dangers of invafion from without, and convulfions within.

He has endeavoured to prevent the population of thefe ftates; for that purpofe obftructing the laws for naturalization of foreigners; refufing to pafs others to encourage their migrations hither, and raifing the conditions of new appropriations of lands.

He has obftructed the adminiftration of juftice, by refufing his affent to laws for eftablifhing judiciary powers.

He has made judges dependent on his will alone, for the tenure of their offices, and the amount and payment of their falaries.

He has erected a multitude of new offices, and fent hither fwarms of officers to harrafs our people, and eat out their fubftance.

He has kept among us, in times of peace, ftanding armies, without the confent of our legiflatures.

He has affected to render the military, independent of, and fuperior to, the civil power.

He has combined with others to fubject us to a jurifdiction foreign to our conftitution, and unacknowledged by our laws; giving his affent to their acts of pretended legiflation:

For quartering large bodies of troops among us:

For protecting them, by a mock trial, from punifhment for any murders which they fhould commit on the inhabitants of thefe ftates:

For cutting off our trade with all parts of the world:

For impofing taxes on us without our confent:

For depriving us in many cafes, of the benefits of trial by jury:

For tranfporting us beyond feas to be tried for pretended offences:

For abolifhing the free fyftem of Englifh laws in a neighbouring Province, eftablifhing therein an arbitrary Government, and enlarging its boundaries, fo as to render it at once an example and fit inftrument for introducing the fame abfolute rule into thefe Colonies:

For taking away our Charters, abolifhing our moft valuable laws, and altering fundamentally the forms of our Governments:

For fufpending our own legiflatures, and declaring themfelves invefted with power to legiflate for us in all cafes whatfoever.

He has abdicated Government here, by declaring us out of his protection, and waging war againft us.

He has plundered our feas, ravaged our coafts, burnt our towns, and deftroyed the lives of our people.

He is, at this time, tranfporting large armies of foreign mercenaries to compleat the works of death, defolation and tyranny, already begun with circumftances of cruelty and perfidy, fcarcely paralleled in the moft barbarous ages, and totally unworthy the head of a civilized nation.

He has conftrained our fellow citizens taken captive on the high feas to bear arms againft their country, to become the executioners of their friends and brethren, or to fall themfelves by their hands.

He has excited domeftic infurrections amongft us, and has endeavoured to bring on the inhabitants of our frontiers, the mercilefs Indian Savages, whofe known rule of warfare, is an undiftinguifhed deftruction, of all ages, fexes and conditions.

In every ftage of thefe oppreffions we have petitioned for redrefs, in the moft humble terms: Our repeated petitions have been anfwered only by repeated injury. A Prince, whofe character is thus marked by every act which may define a tyrant, is unfit to be the ruler of a free people.

Nor have we been wanting in attentions to our Britifh brethren. We have warned them from time to time of attempts by their legiflature to extend an unwarrantable jurifdiction over us. We have reminded them of the circumftances of our emigration and fettlement here. We have appealed to their native juftice and magnanimity, and we have conjured them by the ties of our common kindred to difavow thefe ufurpations, which would inevitably interrupt our connection and correfpondence. They too have been deaf to the voice of juftice and of confanguinity. We muft, therefore, acquiefce in the neceffity which denounces our feparation, and hold them, as we hold the reft of mankind, enemies in war; in peace, friends.

We, therefore, the Reprefentatives of the UNITED STATES OF AMERICA, in GENERAL CONGRESS affembled, appealing to the Supreme Judge of the world for the rectitude of our intentions, do in the name and by the authority of the good people of thefe Colonies, folemnly publifh and declare, That thefe United Colonies are, and of right ought to be, FREE AND INDEPENDENT STATES; that they are abfolved from all allegiance to the Britifh Crown, and that all political connection between them and the State of Great Britain, is and ought to be totally diffolved; and that as FREE AND INDEPENDENT STATES, they have full power to levy war, conclude peace, contract alliances, eftablifh Commerce, and to do all other acts and things which INDEPENDENT STATES may of right do. And for the fupport of this declaration, with a firm reliance on the protection of Divine Providence we mutually pledge to each other our lives, our fortunes, and our facred honour.

Signed by order and in behalf of the Congrefs,

JOHN HANCOCK, Prefident.

ATTEST.

CHARLES THOMSON, Secretary.

NEW-YORK: PRINTED BY JOHN HOLT, IN WATER-STREET.

The Declaration of Independence, printed in the July 11, 1776 issue of John Holt's *New York Journal.*

Intensified

Persecution

In New York City the proclamation of independence was celebrated by the Patriots in a foray of mischief: the large portrait of the King, which had decorated City Hall, was torn down, and the leaden statue of the King in the Bowling Green, erected not long before as a symbol of loyalty and gratitude for repealing the Stamp Act, was demolished and the lead melted to make bullets. The destruction, however, was far from being unanimously sanctioned. Many of the merchants and wealthy citizens were watching with disgust. Some clergymen were so upset by it all that they closed the doors of their churches.

But worse was yet to come. Delegates to the Congress who had objected to Independence, were recalled and new ones were appointed in their place. Governor Franklin of New Jersey, who had opposed Congress, although his father supported the rebels, was sent to jail in Connecticut where he was treated like a common criminal. People loyal to England, suddenly found themselves exposed to renewed and more vicious violence by mobs. They suffered all sorts of personal indignation, often through malicious or insolent acts of mischief perpetrated under the disguise of patriotism. The barbaric practice of tarring and feathering was resumed with a vengeance, and performed on a number of persons suspected of sympathizing with the Crown.

The Declaration of Independence relegated many of the Loyalists, who were wealthy, educated and professional people, into the ranks of the deprived. They were not allowed to sell or buy land, nor in many cases to will their properties. In Pennsylvania, Tory lawyers and notaries public were forced to stop practicing their profession; druggists and apothecaries were forbidden to continue their services. In Connecticut, there were laws prohibiting the writing or speaking out against Congress or against the Connecticut Assembly. Offenders were punished by flogging, imprisonment, or tarring and feathering. Repeat offenders were banished from the state and their property was confiscated.

To frighten Loyalists, the rebels found it necessary to stage public executions, sometimes for minor offences. In Connecticut a man by the name of Moses Dunbar was hanged because someone determined it was time to show that the rebels meant business. Dunbar had converted from the Congregational to the Anglican Church. For that, he was seized by a mob of forty men. Although he was savagely beaten, he refused to join the militia or support the Revolution. He was jailed for fourteen days. Fearing for his life, after his release, he fled to British-held Long Island where he joined one of the Loyalist Provincial regiments. Wanting to get married, he eventually returned home where he was betrayed by a friend and arrested in January 1777. In his pocket his captors found a document from his regiment. The jury of the Superior Court in Hartford found him guilty of treason, and condemned him to death. He was executed on March 19, on a hill at the present site of Trinity College. He died bravely. His last words on the gallows were: "From the very bottom of my heart I forgive all my enemies and earnestly pray God to forgive them all."*

On January 17, 1777 Massachusetts passed a law, making the "Crime of adhering to Great Britain" punishable by death. In Pennsylvania, at the same time, the Patriots compiled a "Black List" of 490 persons accused of high treason. Not all were condemned to death.

Andrew Oliver, a stamp tax collector, is being attacked by a mob. His beautiful mansion on Oliver Street, Fort Hill (outside of Boston), was wrecked. Oliver narrowly escaped with his life.

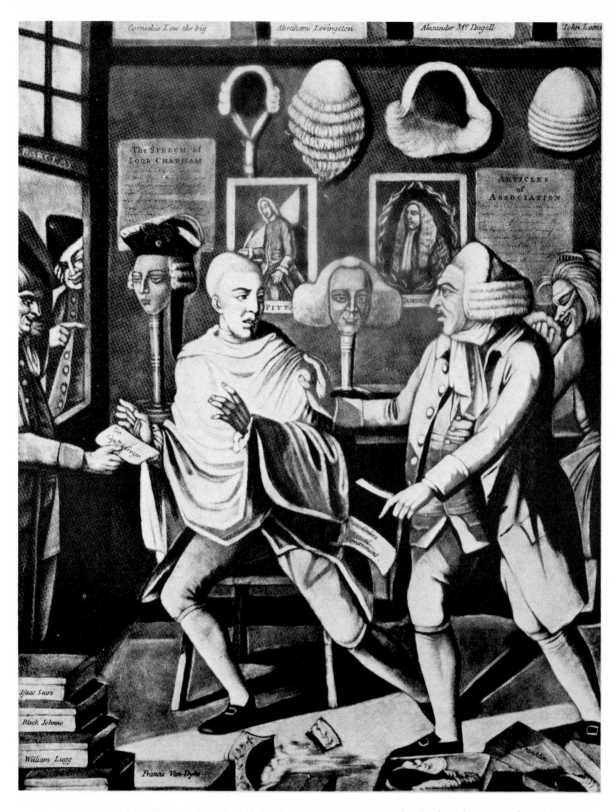

The Patriotic Barber. Having shaved half the face of his customer, the barber discovers that the man is a British captain. Refusing to finish the shave, he chases the captain out of his shop.

A Loyalist, trapped in his house, tries to defend himself against the angry mob.

WE the fubfcribers, being fully fenfible of the bleffings of good government on the one hand, and convinced on the other hand of the evils and calamities attending on tyranny in all fhapes, whether exercifed by one or many ; and having of late feen, with great grief and concern, the diftreffing efforts of a diffolution of all government, whereby our lives, liberties, and properties are rendered precarious, and no longer under the protection of the law, and apprehending it to be our indifpenfable duty to ufe all lawful means in our power, for the defence of our perfons and property, againft all riotous and lawlefs violence, and to recover and fecure the advantages which we are entitled to from the good and wholefome laws of the government; do hereby affociate and mutually covenant and engage to and with each other as follows, viz.

I. That we will, upon all occafions, with our lives and fortunes, ftand by and affift each other in the defence of his life, liberty, and property, whenever the fame fhall be attacked or endangered by any bodies of men, riotoufly affembled upon any pretence, or under any authority not warranted by the laws of the land.

II. That we will, upon all occafions, mutually fupport each other, in the free exercife and enjoyment of our undoubted right to liberty, in eating, drinking, buying and felling, communing and acting what, with whom, and as we pleafe, confiftent with the laws of God and the King.

III. That we will not acknowledge or fubmit to the pretended authority of any Congrefs, Committees of Correfpondence, or other unconftitutional affemblies of men ; but will, at the rifque of our lives, if need be, oppofe the forcible exercife of all fuch authority.

IV. That we will, to the utmoft of our power, promote, encourage, and, when called to it, enforce obedience to the rightful authority of our moft gracious Sovereign, King George the Third, and of his laws.

V. That, when the perfons or property of any one of us fhall be invaded or threatened by any Committees, mobs, or unlawful affemblies, the others of us will, upon notice received, forthwith repair properly armed to the perfon on whom, or place where, fuch invafion and threatening fhall be, and will to the utmoft of our power defend fuch perfon and his property, and, if need be, will oppofe and repel force with force.

A sixteen year old boy from Connecticut by the name of Walter Bates epitomizes the individual bravery displayed by Loyalists in those troubled times. One night he assisted his older brother in rowing to Long Island to join the British army. (Loyalists who wanted to escape from the rebels or join the British forces, used a secret cove where a boat and provisions awaited them.) On his return, the boy was arrested and brought before a local Committee of Safety. He was interrogated, and when nothing could force him to reveal how and from where the Loyalists travelled to Long Island, he was dragged outside the village, stripped of his clothes and tied to a tree. He remained there for over two hours while swarms of mosquitoes drank his blood, and he still refused to talk. His swollen body was then placed on a log in the local sawmill, and his captors threatened to cut him in half. He remained silent. They beat him until he lost consciousness, and finally they dragged him to the nearest town and placed him before a man known as the "hanging judge". He glanced at the boy's swollen face and his pitiful condition and said: "Boy, you have courage. You deserve to be free," and he discharged him.

When the British troops withdrew from Philadelphia in 1778, two Loyalists, Abraham Carlisle and John Roberts, were arrested and tried by a special court with Judge Thomas McKeon presiding. Their offences were helping and soliciting other colonists to enlist in a British regiment. The jury found them guilty of treason but recommended mercy. When the judge sentenced the two men to be hanged, five members of the clergy, several high-ranking military officers, leading patriots, as well as 387 citizens of Philadelphia, signed a petition asking for clemency, but the Executive Council insisted on execution. The hanging was carried out on November 4, 1778 in the presence of Roberts' wife and his ten children.

> At the gallows Carlisle, having been very ill during his confinement, was too weak to say anything, but Mr. Roberts told the people that he suffered for doing his duty to his Sovereign; that his blood would one day be demanded at their hands and then turning to his children, charged and exhorted them to remember his Principles, for which he died . . .*

The rebel leaders justified such public executions as being necessary to set examples to others who refused to join the ranks of the Patriots, and to show the "stability of the new government". In South Carolina, when 700 defeated Scottish Loyalists under Colonel John Boyd were taken prisoners, 70 of them were immediately condemned to death as traitors. Only five were actually executed, the remainder receiving stiff jail sentences.

Around 1778 all available jails were full of Loyalists whose only crime had been their loyalty to the mother country. The worst place of confinement was "Newgate Prison," located in East Granby, Connecticut. It was an old copper mine, sixty feet underground, where prisoners suffered unbelievable hardships. The place was dark, cold, filthy, with water trickling constantly from the top and earth shifting from the sides adding to the misery and the stench of wet bodies.

* Thomas Sharf and Thompson Westcorr: *History of Philadelphia*

A PROSPECTIVE VIEW OF OLD NEWGATE Connecticut's STATE PRISON.

The subterranean Vault, over which this place is built was wrought about the middle of the 17th Century for the purpose of obtaining Copper Ore, the opening into those Gloomy Caverns is a Descent of 35 feet, from thence Descending in various Serpentine Directions 75 Yards, opens to the Well is in depth 74 feet from the Surface to the Water

1. The Commandats apartment 2. the Guard Room 3. the work shop 4. the store for Nails 5. the Bake house 6 the Cole house 7 the Smiths shop 8 the Well 9 the gate for Entrance 10 the Pickets & inclosure of the Prison 11 the path leading from the work shop to the Caverns

Newgate was a prison in Connecticut, commonly known as "Hell". Here Loyalists were chained together and made to work in an underground copper mine.

In 1778 the Massachusetts Assembly passed the "Act of Banishment", and listed over 300 Loyalists who were to be affected by this Act. Not all were wealthy landowners; one third were merchants, another third were farmers, and the rest professional men, artisans and small shopkeepers — in other words, a cross section of the colonial community.

Having boldly seized the reins of government, the new rebel leaders in the country imposed the oath of allegiance on all residents. Those who refused to acknowledge their authority and continued to be loyal to the King, were dealt with swiftly and harshly.

Treks of refugees, heading toward the north, soon became a common sight throughout the thirteen colonies. Loyalists, either banished or driven to desperation, abandoned their homes and, in groups or individually, made their way to Canada where already a few Loyalist settlements had begun to grow.

A loyal servant of the Crown has been tarred and feathered by Patriots.

A mob in New York in the process of toppling the statue of King George III.

Continental paper money, issued by the Continental Congress.

William Franklin, Royal governor of New Jersey, and son of Benjamin Franklin, is arrested by order of the Congress.

View of New York from Governor's Island, 1776.

British Troops in New York

GENERAL HOWE.

General Sir William Howe (1729-1814). He succeeded General Thomas Gage as commander-in-chief of the British forces in North America.

Shortly after the Declaration of Independence, General Howe approached the coast of New York State with a new army. Twenty thousand of his men attacked Long Island and took one thousand American prisoners. Had Howe proceeded with the same vigour as he started out, the whole of Washington's army might have been defeated and the rebellion would have come to an end.

A few weeks later British troops entered New York City which they held until the end of the war. Before the rebels evacuated the city, they attempted to burn it down to deprive the British of the prize they had won. The British soldiers were received with open arms by almost all segments of New York's population, and in particular by frightened Loyalists who had gone into hiding.

However, the Loyalists' enthusiasm and hopes soon turned into bitter disappointment, when they saw how British generals conducted the war in America. Most of the blame for the eventual defeat of the British is to be placed on General Howe who, with his well-equipped army, almost deliberately, let Washington's army escape unmolested to New Jersey. All winter long, instead of pursuing the enemy, he spent his time in New York City in the company of beautiful women, refusing to see anyone who wanted to discuss the war, or much worse, the subject of Loyalists. He actually seemed to hate them. His officers had warned him about these "loyal Americans", supposedly spies and notorious trouble makers. Moreover, the British soldiers did not trust civilians, especially not the disorganized, frightened civilian Loyalists who came to the British army for help.

Edward Winslow, one of the most prominent Loyalists in New York, immediately complained to London about the lack of British co-operation in recruiting Loyalists and providing them with supplies. Loyalist Thomas Jones, an historian of New York, wrote that Howe's proper reward for his service to Britain and to the Loyalists would be execution; and Isaac Wilkins talking to a friend said, "I hope to hear that Howe was hanged".

On instructions from London, General Howe authorized Oliver DeLancey and Courtlandt Skinner to raise four battalions each of Loyalists, and enlist them as auxiliaries to the British units.

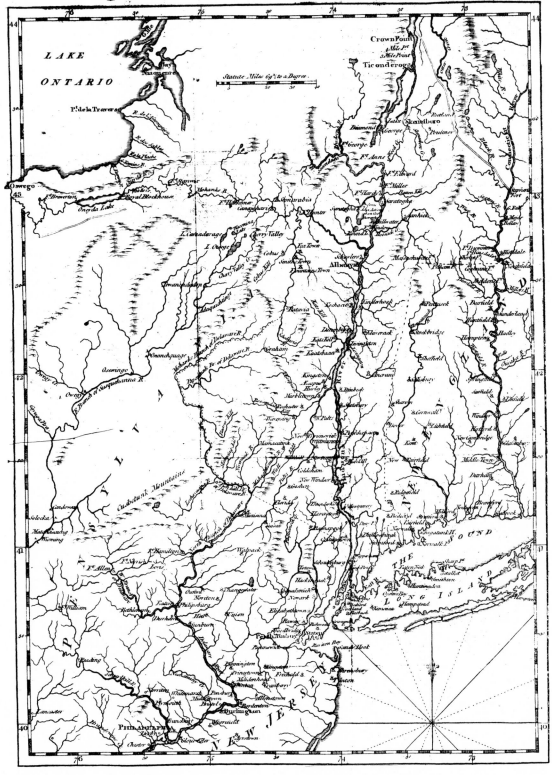

Map of the Hudson River, a strategic waterway during the American Revolution.

Americans attempt to burn the city of New York before the British soldiers enter.

General Washington personally directs the retreat of his troops on Long Island.

Admiral Lord Howe (General William Howe's brother) meets with American representatives Benjamin Franklin, John Adams and Edmund Rutledge on September 11, 1776, on Staten Island to discuss reconciliation. With neither side willing to make concessions, the meeting broke up.

British troops landing at New York.

PROCLAMATION.

By his Excellency, Sir William Howe, Knt. of the Bath, one of his Majesty's Commissioners for restoring peace to the colonies, General, and Commander in Chief of all his Majesty's forces within the colonies lying on the Atlantic Ocean, from Nova-Scotia to West Florida inclusive, &c. &c.

WHEREAS, for the more speedy and effectual suppression of the unnatural rebellion subsisting in North-America, it has been thought proper to levy a number of Provincial troops, thereby affording to his Majesty's faithful and well-disposed subjects, inhabitants of the colonies, an opportunity to co-operate in relieving themselves from the miseries attendant on anarchy and tyranny, and in restoring the blessings of peace and order, with just and lawful government: as a reward for the promptitude and zeal wherewith his Majesty's faithful subjects have entered into the corps now raising, and as a further encouragement to others to follow their laudable example, I do hereby, in consequence of an authority to me given by his Majesty, promise and engage, that all persons who have, or do hereafter enlist into any of the said Provincial corps, to serve for two years, or during the present war in North-America, and shall continue faithful to serve in any of the said corps, agreeable to such their engagements, shall, after being reduced or disbanded, obtain, according to their respective stations, grants of the following quantities of vacant lands in the colonies wherein their corps have been, or shall be raised, or in such other colony as his Majesty shall think fit. Every non-commissioned officer 200 acres; every private soldier 50 acres.

The same to be granted to such of the said non-commissioned officers and soldiers as shall personally apply for the same, by the Governor of the respective colonies, without fee or reward, subject, at the expiration of ten years, to the same quit-rents as other lands are subject to in the province within which they shall be granted, and subject to the same conditions of cultivation and improvement.

Given under my hand, at Head-Quarters, in New-York, the 21st day of April, 1777.

W. HOWE.

General Burgoyne's Expedition

The early part of 1777 was full of activity by government forces with preparations being made for a three-headed campaign to occupy New York State and to isolate New England and particularly Boston, the seat of the rebellion, from the rest of the colonies. General John Burgoyne, who landed in Quebec with nine thousand troops including a large German contingent under General Frederick Riedesel, superseded Guy Carleton as commander.

Early in the summer, Burgoyne was ordered to proceed into New York State by way of Lake Champlain. General Howe, who was at the time in New York City, was to advance up the valley of the Hudson River to join with Burgoyne's army.

General Frederick Riedesel (1738-1800), a German baron and soldier, was sent to America in 1776 as commander of a contingent of German mercenaries lent to the British government by the Duke of Brunswick.

View of the west bank of the Hudson River near Stillwater, N.Y., where Burgoyne's army took post on September 20, 1777.

With Burgoyne's army were two corps of Loyalists consisting of about five hundred men, and a few smaller groups not attached to any regiment. The Queen's Loyal Rangers were under the command of Colonel John Peters, and the King's Loyal Americans were under Ebenezer Jessup, who together with his two brothers, Edward and Joseph, in the fall of 1776 had joined Sir Guy Carleton's army. John Peters, like many other Loyalists, had been arrested and held in prisons at Hartford and Springfield from where he had managed to escape to join the British forces the previous year.

As Burgoyne's army progressed south without much resistance from the rebels, the spirit of the English, and especially the Loyalist forces, remained high. At the start of the campaign, Burgoyne had been assured by his advisers that the population of New York and Vermont would give him spontaneous armed support. The assumption that all colonists in rebel-occupied territory were just waiting for the right moment to fight side by side with the British soldiers proved as wrong as the prediction almost two years earlier that all French Canadians would spontaneously rise and join Benedict Arnold when he invaded Canada to fight the British. The Americans were very much upset by the news that Burgoyne was marching into the colonies with a large force of German soldiers who had been hired by King George as mercenaries. There were also rumours that the Indians employed by the English were frequently left on their own and that some of them were raiding settlements massacring the inhabitants.

View of Fort Edward on the Hudson River, north of Saratoga.

" *Skenesborough-House, July 11.*

" My Lord,

HAVE the honour to acquaint
your Lordship, that the enemy were
dged from Ticonderoga and Mount
ependence on the 6th instant, and were
en on the same day beyond Skenesbo-
h on the right, and to Huberton on
left, with the loss of 128 pieces of
ion, all their armed vessels and bat-
x, the greatest part of their baggage
ammunition, provision and military
es to a very large amount.

Journal of the principal Proceedings.

HAVING remained at Crown-Point
e days, to bring up the rear of the
y, to establish the magazines and the
ital, and to obtain intelligence of the
ny, on

une 30, I ordered the advanced corps,
isting of the British light infantry and
adiers, the 24th regiment, some Ca-
ans and savages, and ten pieces of
t artillery, under the command of
adier-General Frazer, to move from
nam-Creek, where they had been en-
ped some days, up the West shore of
Lake to Four-Mile-Point, so called
being within that distance of the
of Ticonderoga. The German re-
e, consisting of the Brunswick chas-
s, light infantry, and grenadiers, un-
Lieut.-Col. Breymen, were advanced
e same time upon the East shore.

July 1. The whole army made a move-
t forward. Brigadier Frazer's corps
pied the strong post called Three-
e-Point on the West shore; the Ger-
reserve the East shore opposite; the
t wing of the line encamped at Four-
e-Point; the left wing nearly oppo-
on the East shore. The Royal George
Inflexible frigates, with the gun-boats,
anchored just without the reach of
enemies batteries. The rest of the
had been some time without guns,
rder to assist in carrying provisions
Lake Champlain.

The enemy appeared to be posted as
ws: A brigade occupied the old
ch lines upon the height Northward

of the fort of Ticonderoga. These lines
were in good repair, and had several intrenchments behind them, chiefly calcu-
lated to guard the North-West flank, and
they were further sustained by a blockhouse. To the left of these works, about
a mile, the enemy had saw-mills, and a
post sustained by a blockhouse; and another blockhouse, and an hospital, at the
entrance of Lake George. Upon the right
of the French lines, and between them
and the old fort, there were two new
blockhouses, and a considerable battery
close to the water-edge.

" *July 2.* About nine in the morning
a smoke was observed towards Lake
George, and the Indians brought in a
report that the enemy had set fire to their
further blockhouse, and had abandoned
the saw mills; and that a considerable
body were advancing from the lines towards a bridge upon the road which led
to the right of the British camp. A detachment of the advanced corps was immediately put in march under Brigadier
Frazer, supported by a brigade of the line,
and some artillery, under the command
of Major-General Phillips, with orders
to proceed towards Mount Hope, which
is to the North of the lines, to recon-
noitre the enemy's position, and to take
advantage of any post they might abandon or be driven from.

" The Indians under Capt. Frazer, supported by his company of marksmen,
were directed to make a circuit to the left
of Brigadier Frazer's line of march, and
endeavour to cut off the retreat of the
enemy to their lines; but this design mis-
carried through the impetuosity of the
Indians, who attacked too soon, and in

" *July 4.* The army worked hard at their
communications, and got up the artillery,
tents, baggage, and provisions. The enemy at intervals continued the cannonade
upon the camps, which was not, in any
instance, returned.

" The Thunderer radeau, carrying the
battering train and stores, having been
warped up from Crown-Point, arrived
this day, and immediately began to land
the artillery.

" *July 9th and 10th.* The army much
fatigued, many parts of it having wanted
their provisions for two days, almost the
whole their tents and baggage, assembled
in their present position. The right wing
occupies the height of Skenesborough in
two lines, covered on the right flank by
Reidesel's dragoons, *en potence*; the left
flank to Wood Creek. The Brunswick
troops, under Major General Reidesel,
are upon Castletown river, with Breymen's
corps upon the communication of roads
towards Pulteney and Rutland. The regiment of Hesse Hanau are at the head of
East Creek, to preserve the communication with the camp at Castletown, and
secure the batteaux. Brigadier Frazer's
corps is in the center to move on either
wing of the army.

" The remains of the Ticonderoga army are at Fort Edward, where they have
been joined by considerable corps of fresh
troops.

" Roads are opening to march to them by
Fort Anne, and the Wood Creek is clearing of fallen trees, sunken stones, and
other obstacles, to give passage to batteaux,
carrying artillery, stores, provisions, and
camp-equipage. These are laborious
works; but the spirit and zeal of the
troops are sufficient to surmount them.
In the mean time all possible diligence is
using at Ticonderoga to get gun-boats,
batteaux, and provision-vessels, into Lake
George. A corps of the army will be
ordered to penetrate by that route, which
will be afterwards the route of the magazines, and a junction of the whole is intended at Fort Edward.

" I transmit to your Lordship herewith
returns of the killed and wounded, and
lists of such parts of the artillery, provisions, and stores taken from the enemy,
as could be collected in so short a time.
By a written account found in the Com-
missary's house at Ticonderoga, six thousand odd hundred persons were fed from
the magazines the day before the evacuation.

I have the honour to be, &c.

J. BURGOYNE."

Letter from General Burgoyne to Lord George Germaine, the British Secretary of State for
the American Colonies.

General Burgoyne addresses his Indian allies, reminding them to "fight humanely".

General John Burgoyne (1722-1792), nicknamed "Gentleman Johnny" by his soldiers. He expected his officers to treat the soldiers like "human beings" in a day, when brutal corporal punishment was part of their training.

Eighteenth century German dragoon officer.

When Burgoyne reached Fort Edward and Fort George towards the end of July, he had to face two unpleasant facts. His supply line which now stretched over 185 miles, was constantly being interrupted, and he realized that the support he had expected from the Loyalist population was not materializing. To replenish the dwindling stock of horses needed to haul wagons and artillery and obtain new supplies of cattle and carriages, a special expedition to Bennington, Vermont, was organized. Peters' Queen's Loyal Rangers, consisting of 300 men, were chosen for this dangerous mission. The officers of this unit were Captains Justus Sherwood, Jeremiah French, David McFall and Francis Hogel; Lieutenants Gershom French, John Dulmage, James Parrott and Ruben Hawley. Gershom French was Adjutant. There were also 374 Germans, 50 marksmen of Captain Fraser's company, and some Indians. The total strength of the combat force was about 800 men. They were placed under the command of Colonel Friedrich Baum, commander of the Brunswick dragoons and a man who had no knowledge of the English language. As one officer put it, "he could not utter one word of English."

How Burgoyne expected the expedition to succeed under a commanding officer who could not speak English but was supposed to direct surprise raids and try to rally sympathizers to the English side, is not clear. In addition to their language problem, the Germans were unfit for fast raids. Their heavy boots, cumbersome swords and awkward uniforms slowed them down on the road and rendered them almost immobile in the woods.

The Bennington Battle monument at Old Bennington stands 306 feet high.

The Battle of Bennington, August 16, 1777, ended in defeat for the British.

The Bennington battlefield.

Plaques on the grounds of the Bennington battle-field commemorate the events of August 16, 1777.

THE HEAD-PIECE OF THE GRENADIERS' UNIFORM, 1776.

A British grenadier's hat, designed to make him look tall and awe-inspiring to the enemy.

On August 13th, the first advance party of Baum's force came upon the enemy. The Americans were commanded by John Stark who had gathered a large militia force of volunteers to fight the British. When Baum learned that the strength of the enemy was greater than expected, he immediately asked Burgoyne for reinforcements. But it was too late. The Queen's Loyal Rangers fell into a trap devised by Stark. Peters lost half his men in the engagement. Colonel Baum's regular soldiers were treated as prisoners of war, but the Loyalists, 152 of them, were tied in pairs to horses and led away amid the jeers and scoffs of the rebels.

101

Colonel Barry St. Leger (1737-1789) served with the British army in America throughout the Seven Years' War. In the Revolutionary War he led the British expedition against Fort Stanwix in the summer of 1777.

General Horatio Gates (1728-1806) was a British army officer who retired in 1772 to emigrate to Virginia. He became a supporter of the revolutionary cause in the colonies, and in 1775 was appointed adjutant general in the Continental Army.

After the battle at Bennington the remainder of Peters' corps was merged with Jessup's corps and the second battalion of Sir John Johnson's regiment. Colonel Peters received a captaincy under Jessup's command. (Jessup's corps was disbanded in 1783 and settled in the Eastern District.) The failure of the Bennington expedition was the first misfortune in Burgoyne's ill-fated campaign of 1777. Others were soon to follow.

The smallest, yet one of the most important units in Burgoyne's campaign was led by Colonel St. Leger, who with Sir John Johnson and Joseph Brant, went up the St. Lawrence, via Lake Ontario to Oswego and then to the Mohawk Valley. Their mission was to strike through Six Nations territory and join Burgoyne at Albany. The route they took led over a well-established trail to the head of navigation on the Mohawk River. Here at the portage between that river and Wood Creek stood Fort Stanwix, well reinforced with American troops.

On August 7, 1777, Johnson's Greens and Brant's Mohawks rushed toward the enemy. The fighting was hand to hand, resulting in a terrible slaughter and great losses on both sides. General Herkimer, who led the rebel army, was fatally wounded. The defenders of Fort Stanwix were ready to surrender, when Benedict Arnold arrived with fresh American troops, forcing St. Leger and his Loyalists to abandon their position and retreat to Montreal.

In the meantime, General Howe, instead of going north to join Burgoyne, went south to capture Philadelphia. Burgoyne's advance on Albany ended in disaster. The American forces cut off his supplies. His army dwindled day by day. He was left in command of six thousand men, besieged by disease, desertions and hunger. Despondent, he surrendered near Saratoga to General Gates. Shortly before he surrendered, however, he had ordered all Loyalists to try to escape in small groups and find their way to Canada. He knew that he could not protect the Loyalists. British soldiers would be treated by the enemy as prisoners of war, but the Loyalists were marked as traitors, and that meant jail or execution for them. Most of the enlisted men escaped. Colonel John Peters, under great risk, led his party through the enemy's line toward Lake George and thence to Canada. The Jessup brothers stayed with Burgoyne and surrendered. "Desert you we did not", said Ebenezer Jessup. This heroic gesture by the Jessups pleased the rebels so much that they allowed all three brothers to go unmolested to Canada.

Albany, October 20, 1777.

MY LORD,

NO possibility of communication with your Lordship having existed since the beginning of September, at which time my last dispatches were sent away, I have to report to your Lordship the proceedings of the army under my command from that period ;—a series of hard toil, incessant effort, stubborn action, till disabled in the collateral branches of the army by the total defection of the Indians ; the desertion or the timidity of the Canadians and Provincials, some individuals excepted ; disappointed in the last hope of any timely co-operation from other armies ; the regular troops reduced by losses from the best parts, to 3500 fighting men, not 2000 of which were British ; only three days provisions, upon short allowance, in store ; invested by an army of 16,000 men, and no apparent means of retreat remaining ; I called into council all the Generals, Field-Officers, and Captains commanding corps, and by their unanimous concurrence and advice I was induced to open a treaty with Major-General Gates.

Brigadier-Gen. Fraser's corps, sustained by Lieut. Col. Breyman's corps, made a circuit in order to pass the ravin commodiously, without quitting the heights, and afterwards to cover the march of the line to the right : these corps moved in three columns, and had the Indians, Canadians, and Provincials, upon their fronts and flanks. The British line, led by me in person, passed the ravin in a direct line South, and formed in order of battle as fast as they gained the summit, where they waited to give time to Fraser's corps to make the circuit, and to enable the left wing and artillery, which, under the command of Major-General Phillips and Major-General Reidesel, kept the great road and meadows near the river, in two columns, and had bridges to repair, to be equally ready to proceed. The 47th regiment guarded the batteaux.

The danger to which the lines were exposed becoming at this moment of the most serious nature, orders were given to Majors-General Phillips and Reidesel to cover the retreat, while such troops as were most ready for the purpose returned for the defence of them. The troops retreated hard pressed, but in good order. They were obliged to leave six pieces of cannon, all the horses having been killed, and most of the artillery-men, who had behaved, as usual, with the utmost bravery, under the command of Major Williams, being either killed or wounded.

The troops had scarcely entered the camp, when it was stormed with great fury, the enemy rushing to the lines under a severe fire of grape-shot and small arms. The post of the light infantry under Lord Belcarres, assisted by some of the line, who threw themselves by order into those intrenchments, was defended with great spirit ; and the enemy, led on by General Arnold, was finally repulsed, and the General wounded ; but, unhappily, the intrenchments of the German reserve, commanded by Lieutenant-Colonel Breyman, who was killed, were carried, and although ordered to be recovered, they never were so ; and the enemy by that misfortune gained an opening on our right and rear. The night put an end to the action.

103

General Burgoyne reports to London on his ill-fated campaign of 1777.

THE annexed answers being given to Major-General Gates's proposals, it remains for Lieut.-General Burgoyne, and the army under his command, to state the following preliminary articles on their part.

I. The troops to march out of their camp with the honours of war, and the artillery of the intrenchments, which will be left as hereafter may be regulated.

I. The troops to march out of their camp with the honours of war, and the artillery of the intrenchments, to the verge of the river where the old fort stood, where their arms and artillery must be left.

II. A free passage to be granted to this army to Great-Britain, upon condition of not serving again in North-America during the present contest; and a proper port to be assigned for the entry of transports to receive the troops whenever General Howe shall so order.

II. Agreed to for the port of Boston.

III. Should any cartel take place, by which this army or any part of it may be exchanged, the forgoing article to be void, as far as such exchange shall be made.

III. Agreed.

IV. All officers to retain their carriages, bat-horses, and other cattle; and no baggage to be molested or searched, the Lieut.-General giving his honour that there are no public stores secreted therein. Major-General Gates will of course take the necessary measures for the security of this article.

IV. Agreed.

V. Upon the march the officers are not to be separated from their men; and in quarters the officers shall be lodged according to rank; and are not to be hindered from assembling their men for roll-calling, and other necessary purposes of regularity.

V. Agreed to, as far as circumstances will admit.

VI. There are various corps in this army composed of sailors, batteau-men, artificers, drivers, independent companies, and followers of the army; and it is expected that those persons, of whatever country, shall be included in the fullest sense, and utmost extent of the above articles, and comprehended in every respect as British subjects.

VI. Agreed to in the fullest extent.

VII. All Canadians, and persons belonging to the establishment in Canada, to be permitted to return there.

VII. Agreed.

VIII. Passports to be immediately granted for three officers, not exceeding the rank of captain, who shall be appointed by Gen. Burgoyne to carry dispatches to Sir Wm. Howe, Sir Guy Carleton, and to Great-Britain by the way of New-York, and the public faith to be engaged that these dispatches are not to be opened.

VIII. Agreed.

IX. The foregoing articles are to be considered only as preliminaries for framing a treaty, in the course of which others may arise to be considered by both parties; for which purpose it is proposed that two officers of each army shall meet and report their deliberations to their respective Generals.

IX. This capitulation to be finished by two o'clock this day, and the troops march from their encampment at five, and be in readiness to move towards Boston to-morrow morning.

X. Lieut.-General Burgoyne will send his Deputy Adjutant-General to receive Major-General Gates's answer to-morrow morning at ten o'clock.

X. Complied with.

(Signed)   *Horatio Gates.*
Saratoga, Oct. 15, 1777.

Burgoyne's proposed terms of his surrender at Saratoga were presented to General Gates on October 15, 1777.

Gates accepted Burgoyne's proposed terms of surrender on October 17, 1777. "Fortune of war, General Gates, has made me your prisoner", said General Burgoyne, to which Gates replied: "I shall always be ready to testify that it has not been through any fault of your Excellency."

General Burgoyne surrenders his sword to General Gates at Saratoga.

Encampment of the *Convention Army* at Charlottesville, Virginia. Having surrendered at Saratoga by "convention", the prisoners became known as the "Convention Army". They were not sent to Britain as had been agreed upon, but were kept as prisoners of war and shifted from place to place until the end of the Revolutionary War.

Provincial

Regiments

Between the time of General Howe's landing in New York on July 2, 1776 and Burgoyne's march toward Albany in June, 1777, new Loyalist regiments were being organized. Enlistment proceeded slowly. Many loyal colonists hesitated to join the British army, because of the snobbish attitude of British officers who regarded themselves as superior soldiers, and looked upon Americans as "backwoods farmers" without military discipline and training.

This attitude helped to deprive the British of victory at Boston, was a cause of the evacuation of Philadelphia and General Cornwallis' surrender at Yorktown, and contributed in the end to the evacuation of New York and the loss of the war to these "undisciplined, poorly-trained peasants of America", as British officers called them.

The Loyalist regiments became known as Provincial Corps of the British army. At the beginning, they were not expected to do any serious fighting. That was to be the job of the better trained regulars. However, no less than 30,000 Loyalists took up arms, sacrificing their properties and their lives, or enduring untold hardships to manifest their rights which had been taken away by the rebels.

Among the most active Provincial regiments were: the King's Rangers, the Royal Fencible Americans, the Queen's Rangers, the New York Volunteers, the King's American Regiment, the Maryland Loyalists, DeLancey's Battalions, the North Carolina Highland Regiment, the King's American Dragoons, the New Jersey Volunteers, the Pennsylvania Loyalists, and the Guides and Pioneers.

On October 15, 1777, Captain John Graves Simcoe of the British Grenadiers was promoted to Major and was given the command of the Queen's Rangers organized by Major Robert Rogers. This regiment gained distinction for its effective fighting and towards the end of the revolutionary war fought alongside British forces on the north bank of the York River under the command of General Cornwallis.

Colonel John Graves Simcoe (1752-1806) served with the British forces during the American Revolution. He commanded the Queen's Rangers from 1777 to 1781. When Upper Canada came into being in 1791, Simcoe was appointed the province's first Lieutenant-Governor.

The Loyalist Provincials, as a rule, received whatever equipment was left after the British regulars had been served. Loyalists were issued with green coats to distinguish them from the regulars who wore red. By 1778, however, some of the Loyalist corps had demonstrated their worth as soldiers and to honour them they were to be issued with the red coats of the regulars. Some commanders of the Provincials, notably John Graves Simcoe (later Lieutenant-Governor of Upper Canada) objected. They had learned that green was a safer colour as it soon faded and became an excellent camouflage for the soldier!

Before the war was over, there were four categories of regiments involved in the fight against the rebels. British Regulars, American Regulars, Provincial Corps and Militia.

Loyalist regiments were to be found wherever the British army was in control. After Burgoyne's surrender, they were stationed around Montreal, Sorel, Fort St. John and at outpost blockhouses as far south as Point au Fer, on Lake Champlain.

A Queen's Ranger

The Fighting Spirit
of Loyalists

Having been driven from their homes, disarmed and humiliated by rebels, Loyalist leaders like Sir John Johnson, John and Walter Butler, Edward Jessup, John Peters, and Joseph Brant, were eager to obtain rifles and ammunition to fight their foe in the field. Loyalists, whose properties had been confiscated and whose houses were burned to the ground, carried in their hearts a bitter hatred toward their rebellious countrymen and waited for a chance to retaliate.

In the Carolinas, Colonel Banastre Tarleton's Loyal Cavalry and Rawdon's Volunteers of Ireland, with a combined force of 2,400 men, defeated rebel leader General Horatio Gates in a bloody battle. This victory was followed by another engagement in which Tarleton defeated Thomas Sumter and took three hundred prisoners. Banastre Tarleton soon became an anathema to the rebels who called him "Bloody Tarleton," but to the Loyalists he was the legendary hero of the light cavalry. His successful ventures came to an end when he was surrounded by an overwhelming force led by Daniel Morgan. Tarleton's unit suffered heavy losses of fine officers and veteran soldiers and he was able to escape with only one hundred horsemen.

Governor William Tryon of New York zealously conducted raids along the coast of New Jersey, destroying villages in such a punitive and vindictive manner that many of his own subordinates accused him of cruelty.

Perhaps the most destructive and cruelest raids of the revolutionary war were the massacres carried out in the Wyoming and Cherry Valleys. Wyoming Valley stretches about twenty-five miles along the Susquehanna River in the northern part of Pennsylvania. The communities there were peaceful until 1777, when the local Committee of Safety discovered that among the inhabitants were a large number of Loyalist supporters. Consequently, many prominent settlers were arrested and sent to Connecticut where they ended up in the dreaded Simsbury Mines. At home, their families were exposed to constant harassment by the Sons of Liberty. Word of their suffering reached Colonel John Butler and his Rangers, who were stationed at Fort Niagara. They pledged to rescue

Colonel Banastre Tarleton (1754-1833), a daring British officer who had volunteered for service in America, became one of the most feared men in the British army to the rebels. To the Loyalists he was the legendary hero of the light cavalry.

the hundreds of women, children and old people who were at the mercy of the rebels. Butler's Rangers, Johnson's Royal Greens, and a large number of Indians under the command of Giengwahtoh, took part in the expeditions that were to follow. One group of settlers from the Wyoming Valley awaiting trial in Connecticut on suspicion of being Loyalists, managed to escape and join the raiders.

Soon the Wyoming Valley became a scene of total devastation. Repeated raids by the Rangers kept the valley aflame for months, destroying crops and burning homes. They forced many of the rebels' families to leave their farms and seek shelter in the fortified towns of Schenectady and Albany. Similar raids were carried out in Cherry Valley.

Aside from these major retaliatory raids, the Rangers engaged in hundreds of individual forays into settlements along the northern part of New York State. They adopted the Indian way of fighting, approaching a village quietly like "a pack of wolves", often in the night, burning houses or granaries. Before the militia could come to the rescue, the Rangers were far away, safely hiding in the forest and planning their next expedition.

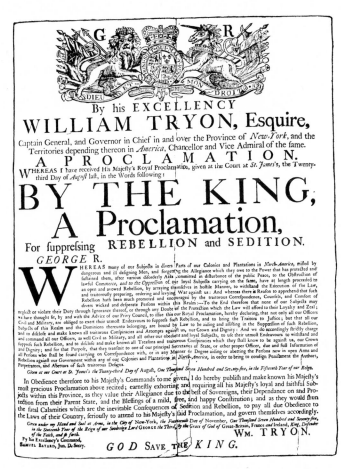

The King's Proclamation to suppress Rebellion and Sedition in the American colonies.

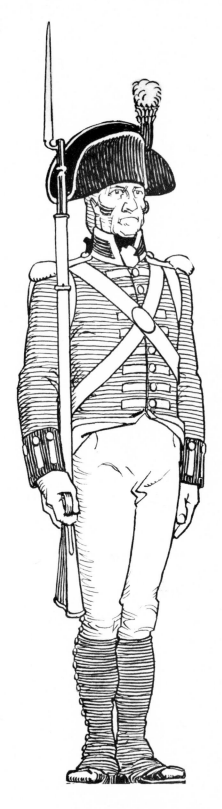

A British private of the eighteenth century.

The Wyoming Valley Massacre. In July, 1778, Butler's Rangers, supported by several hundred Indian warriors, invaded the Wyoming Valley of Pennsylvania. A battle fought in the valley on July 3rd ended in total defeat for the settlers, many of whom were killed, tortured or scalped in the aftermath.

The QUEEN'S RANGERS

1777 Colours
of the Rangers,
now in the Public
Library, Toronto.

Presented to the
City of Toronto
by Col. F.B. Robins

ARTICLES of MILITARY EQUIPMENT

Gilt

Gorget of Col. Fanning King's American Regiment 1776-1783

In Fort Ticonderoga Museum

Silver

Gorget 1770-1796

Lieutenant of Infantry 1796 with Gorget & Single Epaulette

Cross Belt

Right

Left

Belt Plate

Officer's Epaulette

Cartridge Box

Artillery Epaulettes

22½ inches

2nd. Batl. Militia

16 inches

Drum carried by Enoch Goodwin, Westmoreland Militia, N.B. 1776. In Beausejour Museum

C·W·J·

Bayonet Scabbard

Powder Horns used by Militia 1776 +

TEUCRO DUCE NIL DESPERANDUM.

First Battalion of Pennsylvania Loyalists, commanded by His Excellency Sir WILLIAM HOWE, K. B.

ALL intrepid, able-bodied HEROES, who are willing to serve His Majesty King GEORGE the Third, in Defence of their Country, Laws, and Constitution, against the arbitrary Usurpations of a tyrannical Congress, have now not only an Opportunity of manifesting their Spirit, by assisting in reducing their too-long deluded Countrymen, but also of acquiring the polite Accomplishments of a Soldier, by serving only two Years, or during the present Rebellion in America.

Such spirited Fellows, who are willing to engage, will be rewarded at the End of the War, besides their Laurels, with Fifty Acres of Land in any County they shall chuse, where every gallant Hero may retire, and enjoy his Bottle and Lass. [every man Cant officer want require 200 Acres of land]

Each Volunteer will receive, as a Bounty, FIVE DOLLARS, besides Arms, Cloathing and Accoutrements, and every other Requisite proper to accommodate a Gentleman Soldier, by applying to Lieutenant-Colonel ALLEN, or at Captain STEVENS's Rendezvous, in Front-street.

PRINTED by JAMES HUMPHREYS, JUNR. in *Market-street*, between *Front* and *Second-streets*.

Appeal for volunteers to serve in Loyalist regiment.

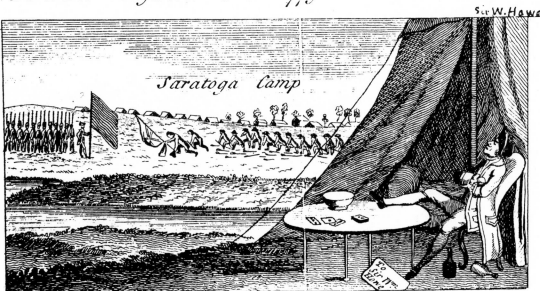

Westminster Magazine. June 1779.

The Generals in America doing nothing, or worse than nothing.

Cartoon, published in England in 1779, accuses General Howe of "doing worse than nothing" while Burgoyne surrenders at Saratoga.

A *Letter from General* LEE *to General* BURGOYNE, *dated Camp on Pro-spect Hill, Dec.* 1.

" Dear Sir,

AS I am just informed you are ready to embark for England, I cannot refrain from once more trespassing on your patience. An opportunity is now presented of immortalizing yourself as the saviour of your country. The whole British Empire stands tottering on the brink of ruin, and you have it in your power to prevent the fatal cata-strophe; but it will admit of no delay. For Heaven's sake avail yourself of the precious moment ; put an end to delu-sion ; exert the voice of a brave virtu-ous citizen, and tell the people at home that they must immediately rescind all their impolitic acts ; that they must overturn the whole frantic system, or that they are undone. You ask me, in your letter, if it is independence at which the Americans aim ? I answer, No ! the idea never entered a single American's head, until a most in-tolerable oppression forced it upon them. All they required was to re-main masters of their own property, and be governed by the same equitable laws which they had enjoyed from the first formation of the colonies. The ties of connection, which bound them to their Parent Country, were so dear to them, that he who would have ven-tured to have touched them, would have been considered as the most im-pious of mortals; but these sacred ties, the same men who have violated or baffled the most precious laws and rights of the people at home, dissipated or re-fused to account for their treasures, tarnished the glory, and annihilated the importance of the nations; these sacred ties, I say, so dear to every American, are now rending asunder.

You ask, whether it is the weight of taxes of which they complain ? I answer, No ; it is the principle they combat, and they would be guilty in the eyes of God and men, of the pre-sent world and all posterity, did they not reject it ; for, if it were admitted, they would have nothing that they could call their own. They would be in a worse condition than the wretched slaves in the West-India Islands, whose little peculium has ever been esteemed inviolate. But wherefore should I dwell on this ? Is not the case of Ireland the same with theirs ? They are subordinate to the British empire, they are subor-dinate to the Parliament of Great-Bri-tain ; but they tax themselves.

I should not, perhaps, be extra-vagant, if I advanced, that all the ships in the world would be too few to tran-sport force sufficient to conquer three millions of people, unanimously deter-mined to sacrifice every thing to liberty; but, if it were possible, the victory would be not less ruinous than the defeat ; you would only destroy your own strength. No revenue can possibly be extracted out of this country. The army of place-men might be encreased, but her cir-cuitous commerce, founded on perfect freedom, (which alone can furnish riches to the metropolis,) would fall to the ground. But the dignity of Great Britain, it seems, is at stake. Would you, Sir, if in the heat of passion you had struck a simple drummer of your regiment, and afterwards discovered it unjustly, think it any forfeiture of your dignity

THE
CONTROVERSY

BETWEEN

Great Britain and her Colonies

REVIEWED;

THE SEVERAL PLEAS OF THE COLONIES,

In Support of their Right to all the Liberties
and Privileges of British Subjects, and to
Exemption from the Legislative Authority of
Parliament,

STATED AND CONSIDERED;

AND

The Nature of their Connection with, and
Dependence on, GREAT BRITAIN,

SHEWN,

UPON THE EVIDENCE OF

HISTORICAL FACTS

AND

AUTHENTIC RECORDS.

_____

LONDON:
Printed for J. ALMON, opposite Burlington-House,
in Piccadilly. MDCCLXIX.

A book, published in England in 1769, examines the colonists' right
to the liberties and privileges as British subjects.

Sir Frederick Haldimand (1718-1791), a Swiss by birth, joined the British army in 1754 and served in America throughout the Seven Years' War. At the outbreak of the American Revolution he was promoted to general, and in 1778 he succeeded Sir Guy Carleton as Governor-in-Chief of Canada, and as such he later directed the settlement of Loyalist refugees in Canada.

Migration to Canada

In the midst of Loyalist activities organizing Provincial regiments and planning raids on rebel-occupied territory, a new Governor General, Sir Frederick Haldimand, arrived in 1778 in Canada to replace Sir Guy Carleton who had requested to be relieved of his post.

Haldimand was a Swiss and a professional soldier in the service of Britain, who had had considerable experience in North America. He had served during the Seven Years' War as a colonel in command of one of the battalions of the Royal American Regiment. He had been at Oswego in 1759, and with General Amherst had taken part in a raid on Montreal in 1760. His first measure of precaution against the Americans was the building of new forts at the upper posts near Prescott, on Carleton Island, and at Niagara. Employing both Loyalists and British soldiers, he strengthened the fortifications at St. John on the Richelieu, erected a new blockhouse on Isle aux Noix, and repaired the fort at Chambly.

Meanwhile, a new tide of Loyalist refugees poured into already crowded places such as St. John, Sorel and Chambly, and people often had to be accommodated in buildings that were not yet completed. Daily rations were stretched so as to be prepared for the needs of unexpected arrivals. Barracks were filled to capacity with people who normally would never have come in contact with each other. Who were these Loyalists? Certainly, not all were rich landowners or government officials, although there were many officials among them who, having taken the oath of allegiance to the King, had steadfastly refused to stain their honour by breaking it. Some of the refugees were lawyers and clergymen. Others were traders and merchants. Among them were graduates from the universities of Yale and Harvard, but the majority of the Loyalists consisted of farmers and townsfolk whose fathers and grandfathers had come from England or Continental Europe, and who had been taught at home and in school to "fear God and honour the King". To uphold their beliefs and remain true to themselves, they were willing to endure hardships and sacrifice all they had. They belonged to different religions, and came from every one of the rebellious colonies and every walk of life. The one thing they had in common was their loyalty to the Crown. They all relied upon the British government and were provided by it with the necessities of life.

In October 1779 New York passed the "Law of Forfeiture", which related to the estates of Loyalists. The following year wives and children of absent Loyalists were forced to leave their homes because the rebel colonies did not wish to support these families; they were evicted under the pretext that the wives were acting as spies. Some of the evicted were assembled in no-man's-land near the border and transferred under a flag of truce to loyal colonies such as Nova Scotia and Quebec. Others made their way on their own to the loyal areas. Carrying what they could of their possessions, they travelled by wagon, on horseback, or plodded on foot. They went down the Richelieu River, or across Lake Ontario, Lake Erie or the Niagara River to reach the settlements already established in Canada (or Quebec, as it was officially called then). A few of the refugee families took along their servants, and some were able to bring a few of their treasured possessions such as a grandfather clock, a chest filled with wedding gifts, tools, homespun clothes or kitchen wares. One woman showed border guards a large tub of lard — food for her family. What the border soldiers did not know was that she had filled the bottom of the tub with most of her money, gold, before pouring hot lard over it!

Once on the British side, the refugees did not always find what they had hoped for. The sick and older people were the ones who suffered most. Food and shelter were deplorable, the future was uncertain, and thoughts of the places they had left, of the houses they had grown up in, made them feel lonely and restless. Neither the government in London, nor General Haldimand were prepared for the mass influx of refugees which literally caught them by surprise. Haldimand did everything in his power to make the new arrivals welcome, and in many instances spent his own money to help the despondent who had lost everything and were seeking his protection.

Loyalist refugees who were placed temporarily in French villages, were subsidized by the government. Most of them were content with life waiting for the outcome of the war, but village residents complained about crowded conditions to which they were subjected for over two years. To ease the situation the government purchased a large tract of land near the mouth of the Richelieu River. Here some of the refugees built their own houses, the cost of which was reimbursed by the government. Major Nairne, who was in charge of the refugees in Verchères (opposite Montreal on the south shore of the St. Lawrence) spent more than twenty thousand pounds within a short time to help establish a new settlement. As the flow of refugees increased, some of the Loyalists went to the remote Gaspé peninsula where their descendants can still be found today.

View of Sorel.

A blockhouse and sawmill of the eighteenth century.

The Section and Plan of a Blockhouse.

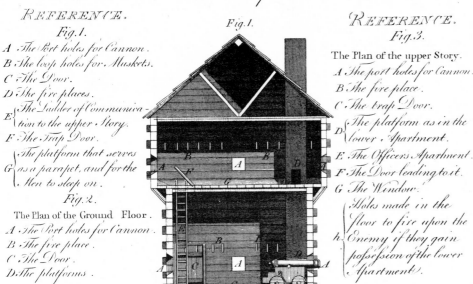

REFERENCE.

Fig. 1.

A. The Port holes for Cannon.
B. The loop holes for Muskets.
C. The Door.
D. The fire places.
E. { The Ladder of Communication to the upper Story.
F. The Trap Door.
G. { The platform that serves as a parapet, and for the Men to sleep on.

Fig. 2.

The Plan of the Ground Floor.

A. The Port holes for Cannon.
B. The fire place.
C. The Door.
D. The platforms.

REFERENCE.

Fig. 3.

The Plan of the upper Story.

A. The port holes for Cannon.
B. The fire place.
C. The trap Door.
D. { The platform as in the lower Apartment.
E. The Officers Apartment.
F. The Door leading to it.
G. The Window.
h. { Holes made in the floor to fire upon the Enemy if they gain possession of the lower Apartment.

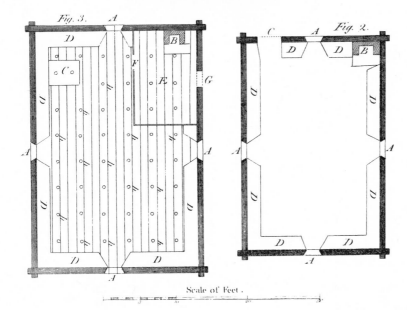

Scale of Feet.

BLOCK
HOUSES

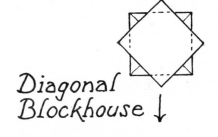

Diagonal
Blockhouse ↓

121

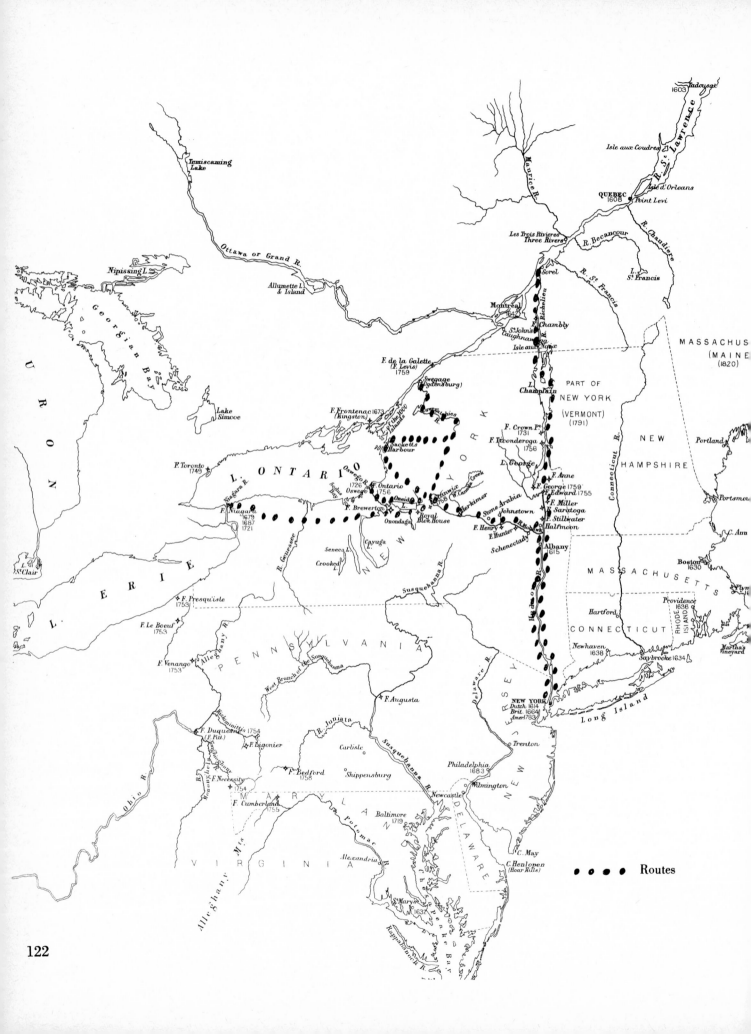

Routes

Loyalists travelling to settlements in Canada.

123

Weary Loyalist refugees pitch a tent in the wildnerness to rest for the night.

Peace Without Honour

The Revolutionary War for the Independence of the United States of America actually came to an end at Yorktown, Virginia. On October 19, 1781, Lord Cornwallis, outnumbered by the combined forces of Washington's army and his French allies under Rochambeau, surrendered. There was still a large British army under Sir Henry Clinton in New York, which made a last desperate attempt to rescue Cornwallis' trapped forces. Clinton embarked with seven thousand men, but when he arrived off Cape Virginia he learned that Lord Cornwallis had capitulated five days earlier. Great Britain had no heart to continue a war which, from the beginning, had been unpopular with her people. The English generals conducting this war did not deserve praise, but rather stern disciplinary action, for their many blunders and their indolence.

After the capitulation, General Washington refused to treat the Loyalists who had fought with Cornwallis' army on the same terms as the British regulars. To Washington the Loyalists were not soldiers but traitors who deserved harsh punishment. To avoid further tragedy, Cornwallis managed to smuggle out a large number of Loyalists on a ship of war which was allowed to sail to New York with the message of the capitulation.

In London, England, the news of Cornwallis' defeat caused gloom and despair. The Secretary of War, Lord George Germaine, resigned, and Sir Guy Carleton was appointed as the Commander-in-Chief in America as reward for his previous services.

In the meantime Washington returned with his army from Yorktown to New York State. However, no attempt was made to capture New York City. Washington knew that his army was exhausted.

By now both sides were glad to look for a peaceful solution which would terminate the war by recognizing the independence of the former colonies. Holland was the first foreign country to recognize the new United States of

America. The provisional articles of peace between England and the States were signed on November 30, 1782.

During the peace negotiations England showed a generous attitude towards her former enemy, but generally failed to emphasize the rights of Loyalists and their dependants who fought for the unity of the empire and lost everything including, in some instances, their lives. Loyalists certainly expected some kind of support from Great Britain, having taken up arms on the invitation of England's government and her generals. Moreover, the revolutionary war was not of their making but could more readily be blamed on the short-sightedness of a clique of aristocrats, and the stupidity of some British Parliamentarians who succeeded in denying the colonists their basic rights and privileges as free British subjects. Criticizing England for her lack of concern for the Loyalists, *Rivington's Gazette* of New York wrote: "Even robbers, murderers, and rebels are faithful to their fellows and never betray each other". England's answer to mounting criticism was, "We had but the alternative either to accept the terms proposed, or continue the war".

Lord Cornwallis (1738-1805). As a British statesman, Charles Cornwallis had opposed Parliament's policies that led to the American Revolution. As a British general, he fought in many of the major battles of the Revolutionary War. He was in command of the British troops in the south when the war drew to a close in the fall of 1781.

According to the provisional peace treaty, Congress agreed to recommend to the individual states that Loyalists should be given the opportunity to recover their confiscated properties. However, the clause in the treaty had little meaning since Congress had no power to compel any state to alter its laws. Patriots once again organized special committees for the sole purpose of preventing Loyalists from returning to their former homes, and from recovering their confiscated properties, thus dashing the Loyalists' hopes for any recompense.

However, the loud outcry of destitute Loyalists awakened a spirit of compassion and understanding. Thanks to Sir Guy Carleton, who personally pleaded with the British government on behalf of the deserted Loyalists, and to General Haldimand who vividly described the plight of the refugees in Canada, the situation soon changed for the better. It was decided that Loyalists who had taken up arms in defense of unity and those who had suffered prosecution and had to leave their homes to seek shelter under the British Crown, as well as those who preferred to live in Canada, should be compensated with land and money and be given the necessities of life.

SURRENDER OF CORNWALLIS.

Surrounded by Continental forces, General Cornwallis surrendered at Yorktown, Virginia, to General Washington on October 19, 1781.

British cannon of the Revolutionary War are mounted inside a monument erected on the "Surrender Field" at Yorktown.

View of the "Surrender Field", Yorktown, Virginia, where the American Revolution came to a close.

Monument, erected at the entrance to the site where Lord Cornwallis surrendered his forces.

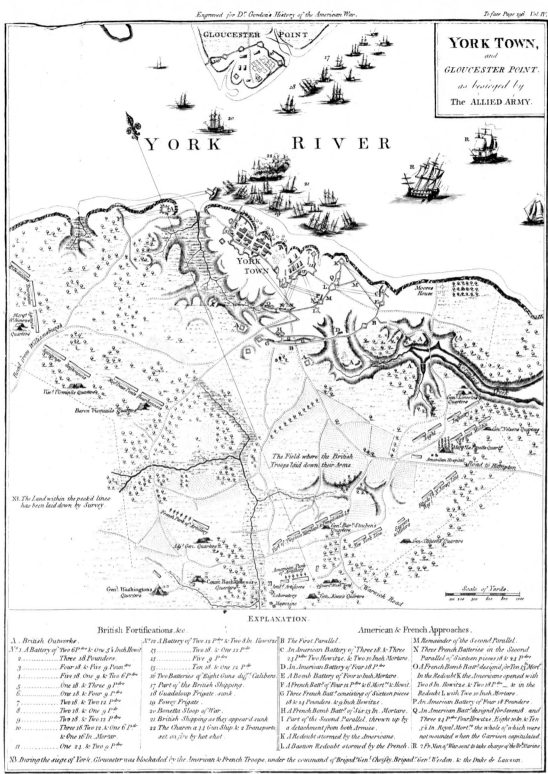

GLOUCESTER POINT

YORK TOWN,
and
GLOUCESTER POINT.
as besieged by
The ALLIED ARMY.

Y O R K   R I V E R

YORK TOWN

Moores House

N.3. The Land within the peck'd lines has been laid down by Survey.

The Field where the British Troops laid down their Arms.

Road to Hampton

Gen.¹ Washington's Quarters.

Warwick Road

Scale of Yards

EXPLANATION.

British Fortifications, &c.

A . British Outworks .
Nᵒ 1. A Battery of Two 6 Pᵈˢ & One 5½ Inch Howit.
2 .... Three 18 Pounders .
3 .... Four 18. & Five 9 Poun.ᵈˢ
4 .... Five 18. One 9. & Two 6 Pᵈˢ
5 .... One 18. & Three 9 Pᵈˢ
6 .... One 18. & Four 9 Pᵈˢ
7 .... Two 18. & Two 12 Pᵈˢ
8 .... Two 18. & One 9 Pᵈˢ
9 .... Two 18. & Two 12 Pᵈˢ
10 .... Three 18. Two 12. & One 6 Pᵈˢ & One 16 In. Mortar .
11 .... One 24. & Two 9 Pᵈˢ

Nᵒ 12. A Battery of Two 12 Pᵈˢ & Two 8 In. Howitze.
13 .... Two 18. & One 12 Pᵈˢ
14 .... Five 9 Pᵈˢ
15 .... Ten 18. & One 12 Pᵈˢ
16 Two Batteries of Eight Guns diff.ᵗ Calibers .
17 Part of the British Shipping .
18 Guadaloup Frigate . sunk .
19 Fowey Frigate .
20 Bonetta Sloop of War .
21 British Shipping as they appeard sunk
22 The Charon a 44 Gun Ship & 2 Transports. set on fire by hot shot .

American & French Approaches .

B The First Parallel .
C An American Battery of Three 18. & Three 24 Pᵈˢ Two Howitze. & Two 10 Inch Mortars.
D An American Battery of Four 18 Pᵈˢ
E A Bomb Battery of Four 10 Inch Mortars .
F A French Batt.ʸ of Four 12 Pᵈˢ & 6 Mort.ˢ & Howit.
G Three French Batt.ˢ consisting of Sixteen pieces 18 & 24 Pounders . & 9 Inch Howitze.
H A French Bomb Batt.ʸ of Six 13 In. Mortars.
I Part of the Second Parallel, thrown up by a detachment from both Armies .
K A Redoubt stormed by the Americans .
L A Bastion Redoubt stormed by the French

M Remainder of the Second Parallel .
N Three French Batteries in the Second Parallel of Sixteen pieces 18 & 24 Pᵈˢ
O A French Bomb Batt.ʸ designd for Ten 13 Mort. In the Redoubt K the Americans opened with Two 8 In. Howitze. & Two 18 Pᵈˢ — & in the Redoubt L with Two 10 Inch Mortars .
P An American Battery of Four 18 Pounders .
Q An American Batt.ʸ designd for Seven 18 . and Three 24 Pᵈˢ Four Howitze, Eight 10 In. & Ten 5½ In. Royal Mort.ˢ the whole of which were not mounted when the Garrison capitulated .
R 2 Fr. Men of War sent to take charge of the Br. Marine .

N.3. During the siege of York, Gloucester was blockaded by the American & French Troops, under the command of Brigad.ᵉ Gen.¹ Choisy, Brigad.ᵉ Gen.¹ Weedon, & the Duke de Lauzun.

T. Conder Sculp.ᵗ London .

Map of the siege of Yorktown

The Loyalists' Last Stronghold

In the spring of 1782 Sir Guy Carleton was recalled from his self-imposed retirement in England and arrived in New York City to replace Sir Henry Clinton as military Governor. At the same time rumours reached North America that Britain was about to recognize the independence of the thirteen colonies as the United States of America. Stunned at first, the mood of the Provincials turned mutinous and some toyed with the notion of carrying on the fight alone. However, without equipment and supplies this was out of the question.

To their dismay, the Loyalists learned that Great Britain found herself unable to carry on the war in America. During the summer of 1782, preliminary peace negotiations got underway in Paris, and soon any hopes of getting a reasonable settlement for the Loyalists were dashed. The British government was in no position to obtain any concessions from the rebellious colonists, on behalf of the people who had lost everything by supporting unity with the mother country. This news crushed many a strong man and left him with the feeling that he had been betrayed.

Loyalists everywhere abandoned their properties, and together with troops of the British, German and Provincial regiments, they sought shelter in the last British stronghold, New York City. Among the remnants of the Provincials were the New Jersey Volunteers, the Maryland Loyalists, the New York Volunteers, the Royal Pioneers, DeLancey's first and second battalions, the Pennsylvania Loyalists, and the Queen's Rangers.

A party of five hundred prospectors sailed to Nova Scotia in October of 1782, to explore the situation at Halifax and in the Annapolis Valley, and they also went up the St. John River from the Bay of Fundy. Some of those who returned published glowing reports of their findings in *Rivington's Gazette* of New York.

In the spring of 1783, a large-scale exodus of Loyalists began from the United States. The first fleet of ships to leave New York carried over seven thousand men, women and chil-

Sir Henry Clinton (1738-1795) was commander-in-chief of the British forces in North America from 1778 until 1782. He fought at the Battle of Bunker Hill, and was knighted for his part in the Battle of Long Island. In 1779 he led an expedition to South Carolina and in the spring of 1780 he captured Charleston. Soon after the surrender of British forces at Saratoga, Clinton was replaced by Sir Guy Carleton, and he returned to England.

dren. New York's harbour was busy all summer and autumn with ships plying to and fro, carrying colonists to the St. John River, to Annapolis, Port Roseway and Fort Cumberland. By the end of that year more than thirty-five thousand Loyalists had left New York for Nova Scotia and New Brunswick. Another contingent consisting of a few hundred people in the charge of Captain Michael Grass, and Captain VanAlstine, departed for Sorel, Quebec. War ships left carrying German and British soldiers back to Europe. On November 25, 1783, the last ship with British regulars, and the remainder of the Loyalists, sailed from New York harbour. The city was immediately occupied by rebel soldiers who, led by General Knox, marched through the streets, loudly cheered by the people of New York. General George Washington came next, on horseback, good looking and in a holiday mood. He and Carleton did not meet on that historic day. General Guy Carleton was preparing to leave New York and sailed on the *Ceres* on November 29. Three years later he was to return again as Lord Dorchester to guide the destiny of Canada.

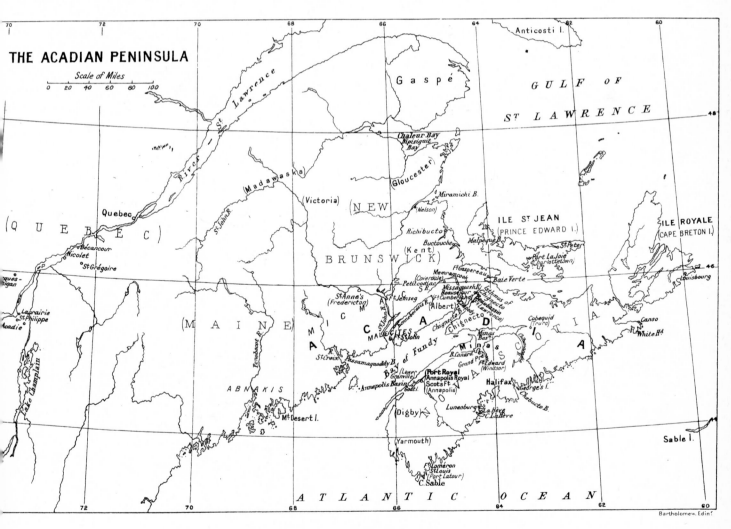

Map of the Acadian Peninsula

The Loyalists who went to Quebec originated mostly from New York, Pennsylvania and the New England provinces. They were mainly backwoods farmers, handy with the axe, the plough and other tools. This type of pioneer had been flocking to Quebec during the war, and many had settled around Montreal when Burgoyne's army was defeated. At the end of the war, many more Loyalists followed the well-travelled Lake Champlain-Richelieu River route into Canada. About ten thousand of the refugees settled along the north side of the St. Lawrence River above Montreal, on the Bay of Quinte shore, in the Niagara region, and east of Detroit. The majority of the latest arrivals consisted of disbanded soldiers and their families of the different Provincial regiments — Johnson's, Jessup's and Butler's Rangers, and all the others who had fought alongside the British against the revolutionaries.

There were disbanded German, Swiss and Dutch soldiers who had enlisted in the British army and who were now entitled along with the loyal Americans, to free land grants for their services. There were the Indians led by brilliant Chief Brant of the Six Nations Confederacy, who had remained loyal to the British Crown. There were Quakers and Mennonites who had refused to take up arms because of their religious convictions. And there were those who went to Canada because they were attracted by the offer of free lands.

American Loyalists are welcomed in England.

Preparations For The Settlement Of Loyalists

When Canada's Governor Frederick Haldimand was informed of the signing of a preliminary peace treaty at Paris on November 30, 1782, he started at once to make preparations for the resettlement of the Loyalists who had been waiting for the outcome of the war in camps at Sorel, Quebec, Three Rivers, Montreal, and Chambly. His first thought was to settle them in the Maritime provinces where already some of the Loyalists had established themselves, and to leave the western part of Quebec, which is now Ontario, to the Mohawks and other Indian tribes.

On May 26, 1783, Haldimand told Sir John Johnson that the Indians who had supported the British Crown against the rebels and who had settled temporarily at Lachine at the close of the Revolutionary War, were discontented with their present situation and were becoming very impatient. They wanted to move and settle where they could build permanent homes. Considering the Bay of Quinte area and further west as the best place for the Indians to settle, Haldimand instructed Major Samuel Holland, the surveyor-general, to proceed immediately to Cataraqui (Kingston) to examine that place, and the country further up the lake, and to find a suitable site for the Mohawks. He asked Joseph Brant and a few of his people to accompany Major Holland to Cataraqui and inspect the site of their future settlement.

Major Samuel Holland, Surveyor General

Haldimand's plan was changed, however, with the unexpected arrival of two reports. Sir Guy Carleton, Commander-in-Chief of the British forces in America, notified him from New York City that a group of Loyalist settlers under Captain Michael Grass and Captain VanAlstine had sailed from there, and wished to be located in the vicinity of Cataraqui or on the Bay of Quinte. (Captain Grass once had been a prisoner at Fort Frontenac at Cataraqui and knew the area well.) The other report came from a survey party along the St. Lawrence River and the Bay of Quinte shore. It described the land there as highly suitable for farming. Haldimand came to the conclusion that Indian and non-Indian Loyalists under these conditions could live side by side to their mutual benefit, and he decided to settle them both there.

Sir John Johnson

Together with Sir John Johnson, who in the meantime had become minister of Loyalists and Indian Affairs in Canada, Haldimand approached the Mississauga Indians to purchase a tract of land between the Gananoque and the Trent Rivers. He then ordered Major John Ross, the Commander of Oswego, to go to Cataraqui and construct temporary barracks for the expected Loyalists.

Major Ross in a way may be regarded as the founder of Kingston. He left Oswego in the summer of 1783 to establish a military post on the site of the abandoned Fort Frontenac at Cataraqui. In 1758, during the Seven Years' War between the British and the French, Fort Frontenac had been destroyed by Colonel John Bradstreet thus ending a colourful era of French rule at Cataraqui. Rather than restore Cataraqui, which became just an outpost, the British chose Carleton Island, nearer the opposite shore, to build a fort and a dockyard. It was there that many Loyalists sought refuge during the American Revolution. Some of them had crossed to Cataraqui and stayed either to trade with the Indians or to work the land that once had been cleared by the French. Eventually, by the Treaty of Paris, Carleton Island was ceded to the United States, so the British had to make preparations to leave.

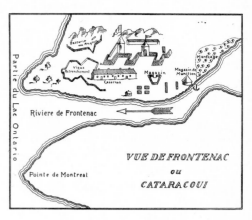

Fort Cataraqui

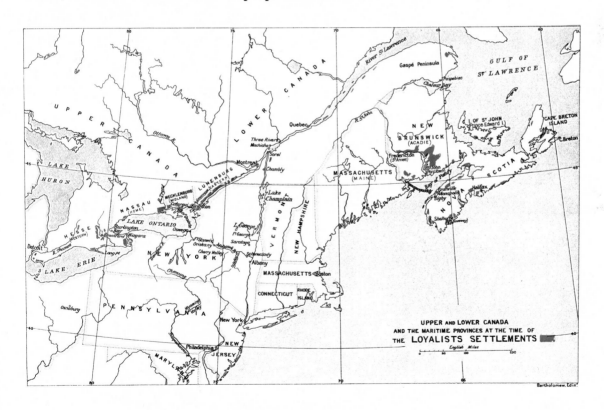

Loyalist settlements in Upper and Lower Canada, and in the Maritime Provinces after the American Revolution.

Major Ross arrived at Cataraqui on July 20, 1783 with a detachment of 25 officers and 422 men from four different regiments. He restored some of the old buildings and erected new barracks inside the walls of the fort. In a letter to Haldimand he proposed to build a mill five miles up the Cataraqui River. The restored fort was called Tête-de-Pont, a name which remained in use until the late 1930's, at which time it once more was officially designated as "Fort Frontenac".

Attached to the Cataraqui post in 1783 was deputy surveyor-general Collins who, under surveyor-general Major Holland, laid out the original town plot of Kingston and whose name is perpetuated at Collins Bay. The site of what was the first survey post in Upper Canada is marked by a cairn in Kingston's City Park:

> To commemorate the planting of the first survey post under Civil Authority in Ontario on 27th October, 1783, by John Collins, Deputy Surveyor General. This survey was undertaken to provide land for the United Empire Loyalists.

Another early inhabitant of Kingston was Ensign James Peachey who left some valuable sketches of Cataraqui. These are the only pictorial record of that time and place, and they are now kept at the Public Archives of Canada. The building on a wharf near the fort, shown in one of the drawings, was the trading post and general store of Richard Cartwright Jr. and John Hamilton. There were also John Howell, a sutler, and Peter Clark, a merchant from Montreal, and Lieutenants John Howard and Oliver Church; together, this small group of residents made up the nucleus of a settlement on the site of the future city of Kingston before the main body of Loyalists came.

In September of 1783 a small advance party of Loyalists from Sorel arrived at Cataraqui, to examine the land and report to the prospective settlers on the conditions and the progress of preparations. Among them were Captain Justus Sherwood, and Captain Michael Grass who was the leader of the Loyalists from New York. Grass returned to Sorel that fall to give an account of his findings, while seventeen men from his company remained to winter at Cataraqui. They were joined by men from the second battalion of the King's Royal Regiment of New York and their families.

Captain Sherwood, after staying for a few days at Cataraqui, organized a survey party and went down the St. Lawrence River to a place called New Johnstown (now Cornwall). Here he found a few refugee squatters, who had come some time ago from New York, Pennsylvania and Connecticut. They had erected shanties not far from the river and had cultivated small portions of land. In his report to General Haldimand, Sherwood described the land as suitable for farming and pointed out that there were a number of good mill sites in the area.

Another survey party, headed by Lieutenant Gershom French of Jessup's Corps, explored the land along the Rideau and Gananoque Rivers. To assist French in his exploratory work the government had provided him with a dozen men from different Loyalist corps, and two natives to guide them through the wilderness. Lieutenant French and his party started at the Ottawa River and followed the Rideau River and Lakes until they reached the source of the Gananoque River. Following this river, they came to the place now occupied by the town of Gananoque. French reported that "from the mouth of the Rideau to its head, a distance of at least eighty miles, the lands are good on both sides of the River and may be all cultivated except a few swamps and stony ridges . . .", but that "the land along the Gananoque was entirely too rocky to cultivate". He added, however, that "there were good mill sites". His observation concerning the land proved accurate when the area was being settled. Lieutenant French himself eventually settled near Côteau du Lac, east of what is now the city of Cornwall.

A view of the ruins of the Fort at Cataraqui

View on the St. Lawrence River

The St. Lawrence River above Gananoque.

139

Pre-Loyalist

Settlements

At the time the Loyalists prepared to travel to their destinations on the St. Lawrence River to take possession of their land grants and build new communities, not all of Upper Canada was a complete wilderness. Some of the native Indian tribes had well-kept villages with gardens fenced against wild animals, and there were already two well-developed permanent white settlements.

The first of these settlements was located on the Detroit River, where the city of Detroit now stands. Here, long before the outbreak of the Seven Years' War, the French had established themselves. It started out as a small fur trading post, and as time went on it became necessary to convert it into a military post. Men were needed to defend the fort, and these soldier-settlers began to work the land and grow their food. The fort was named Pontchartrain in honour of the French Minister of Marine, and under its protection the settlement continued to grow and spread on both sides of the river.

On the Canadian side the settlement began to expand in 1734, when numerous land grants were made to prospective French settlers and to ex-soldiers from the fort. These land grants were laid out in long narrow strips, with the narrow end fronting on the Detroit River between Amherstburg and Sandwich. Houses were built similar to those in Quebec, and a grist mill as well as a blockhouse were constructed. When the British conquered Canada, this settlement on the east bank of the Detroit River already had several hundred inhabitants.

The second settlement in Upper Canada developed at Niagara in the early stages of the Revolutionary War when Butler's Rangers were defending the border, and wives and children came to join their soldier-husbands and fathers. The first white settlers in this area, of course, had been the French, who came with explorer La Salle, and in 1679 began to cultivate the land on the west side of the Niagara River, planting some vegetables for those who remained. The first stockade at the present site of Fort Niagara was built in 1678. It burned two years later. Denonville, the French Governor at the time, erected a fort in 1687, but it was soon abandoned. With the permission of the Senecas, a stone fort was built in 1749 on the spot where Fort Niagara now stands, on the east side of the Niagara River near Lake Ontario.

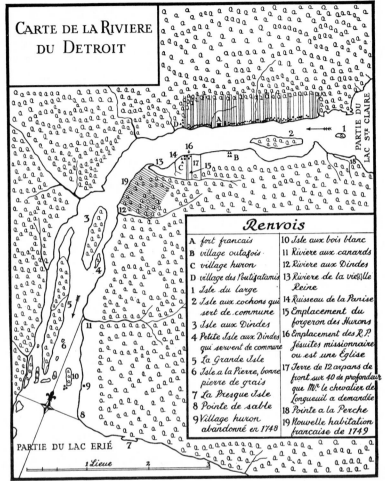

CARTE DE LA RIVIERE DU DETROIT

PARTIE DU LAC STE CLAIRE

PARTIE DU LAC ERIÉ

1 Lieue

Renvois

A fort francais
B village outaſois
C village huron
D village des Poutiſatamis
1 Isle du large
2 Isle aux cochons qui sert de commune
3 Isle aux Dindes
4 Petite Isle aux Dindes qui servent de commune
5 La Grande Isle
6 Isle a la Pierre, bonne pierre de grais
7 La Presque Isle
8 Pointe de sable
9 Village huron abandonné en 1748

10 Isle aux bois blanc
11 Riviere aux canards
12 Riviere aux Dindes
13 Riviere de la vieille Reine
14 Ruisseau de la Panise
15 Emplacement du forgeron des Hurons
16 Emplacement des R.P. Jésuites missionnaire ou est une Eglise
17 Terre de 12 arpans de front sur 40 de profondeur que Mr. le chevalier de Longueuil a demandée
18 Pointe a la Perche
19 Nouvelle habitation francaise de 1749

Map of the Detroit River

Fort Niagara

Chief Joseph Brant and his Mohawks at the Grand River.

A view of Niagara from the heights near Navy Hall.

During the Revolutionary War thousands of white and Indian Loyalist refugees who were driven from their homes, passed through Niagara on their way to other destinations. Many a regiment was quartered here, and expedition after expedition under the commands of Colonel Butler, Sir John Johnson, Guy Johnson, Chiefs Brant and Deserontyou, went out from here to penetrate deep into rebel territory.

In 1778, when the tide of Loyalist refugees swelled, some decided to stay and build shelters. Governor Haldimand suggested to Lieutenant-Colonel Masson Bolton, commander of Fort Niagara, that "considering the great expense and difficulty attending the Transport of Provision to the upper Posts," the commander might want to cultivate land and grow food for the settlers and soldiers. The advice was followed, and settlers were given simple tools and seeds. Sixty bushels of wheat and oats were planted, and also a barrel of Indian corn. Peter and James Secord began the construction of a grist and sawmill. Haldimand promised to forward the necessary machinery, and to send Sergeant Brass to assist in assembling it and to help with the construction of a dam. When the mill was installed fourteen months later, it did not function. The Loyalists, who by now had plenty of wheat on hand, resorted to the domestic method of reducing the grain to powder with a portable mill. The wheat was placed on a flat stationary stone, with a second revolving stone on top; the kernels were crushed between the stones and later sifted through finely woven baskets. This method consumed much time and required very hard labour.

On August 25, 1782, Colonel Butler took the first census of the settlement at Niagara. Besides the two Secord brothers, Peter and James, there was another brother, John. Altogether sixteen families, a total of eighty-three persons, lived at Niagara at that time. Among them were: George Stuart, George Fields, John Depue, Daniel Rowe, Elijah Phelps, Philip Bender, Samuel Lutz, Michael Showers, Harmonious House, Thomas McMicking, Adam Young and Isaac Dolson. The second census, taken in 1783, shows that the number of families had increased to forty-six. There were at that time forty-four houses and twenty barns. Within a short time, the Loyalists had cleared 713 acres of land.

Although the settlement of Loyalists around Niagara had been approved by the government, the settlers had no legal rights to the land they cultivated until May 9, 1781. That day, at a meeting at Niagara between British officials and Mississauga Indians, the land lying west of the Niagara River, four miles in width, was purchased "for the use of His Majesty's faithful subjects". In the spring of 1784, Butler's Rangers were disbanded. The loyal soldiers were supplied with seeds, mills, ploughs, and other implements of husbandry which were furnished gratis. The Niagara forest rang with the sound of the axe chopping trees. Light struck the rich soil. Log cabins rose, and the smoke from their chimneys began drifting along the river.

Major Robert Rogers (1731-1795). He was born in Methuen, Massachusetts. During the Seven Years' War he organized and commanded a number of companies. At the outbreak of the American Revolution he formed the Queen's Rangers, and in 1779 he organized the King's Rangers.

Rangers

Loyalists Journey to New Settlements

Early in the spring of 1784, a notice appeared in the *Quebec Gazette* instructing all Loyalists and disbanded soldiers who wished to obtain land around Oswegatchie (Prescott) and Cataraqui (Kingston) to assemble at the departure points of Quebec, Sorel and Lachine.

By then there were three categories of Loyalist refugees in Canada. The first group were the so-called "incorporated" Loyalists who had been organized in New York by General Carleton and were sent to Canada as settlers under military supervision. The second group consisted of disbanded soldiers from the various Provincial regiments and their dependents, while the third group, known as "unincorporated" Loyalists, was made up of the refugees who had come to Canada independently during the Revolutionary War.

During the preceding winter a party of men had been employed at Lachine to build a special type of flat-bottomed boat known as bateau, which would be suitable to carry the Loyalists up the St. Lawrence River to their destinations. At that time, the chief means of transportation in Upper Canada was by water. Roads did not exist and Indian pathways were dangerous to use on account of hostile Indians and wild animals. Canoes, made from elm or birch bark, were the chief conveyance for individuals or small groups of people. Using a chain of rivers and lakes connected by streams and portages, travellers in the summer would reach most destinations faster by water than by land. The most commonly used routes of travel were the St. Lawrence River, Lake Ontario, the Trent River system and the Ottawa River.

Prior to the arrival of the Loyalists in Upper Canada, soldiers stationed at the forts of Cataraqui, Niagara and Detroit, were the principal travellers, using bateaux of thirty to forty feet in length. The Durham boat came into use on the St. Lawrence a few years later. This kind of boat, also of flat-bottomed construction, with a slip keel, rounded bow, and square stern, measured from eighty to ninety feet and could carry ten times as much cargo as the bateau.

Uniforms of British regulars

Settlers coming to Upper Canada from Montreal by way of the St. Lawrence River, found the journey strenuous. One bateau accommodated four or five families. Twelve boats constituted a brigade, with a conductor in charge of each brigade. The conductor's job was to give directions for the safe passage through the rapids and the treacherous currents. Crew members frequently would have to go ashore and tow the boats with ropes while others would steer them.

The departure of Loyalists from Sorel in 1784 had been delayed on account of a cold winter and heavy ice on the St. Lawrence River. Some of them arrived at Lachine already bone-weary and exhausted after months of preparations and the discomfort of camp life. They were looking forward to settling on the land that had been designated for them. By June, 1784, all Loyalists were assembled and the first group embarked on their journey west. From Lachine, a great flotilla of bateaux carried hundreds of settlers to their destinations to build a new province which would soon be known as Upper Canada.

Durham boats ascending the St. Lawrence River

Survey of Townships

When spring arrived in 1784, the survey of townships along the St. Lawrence River and the Bay of Quinte, begun the previous year, resumed with full speed to accommodate the settlers; they were already on their way, or were preparing to leave the temporary camps at Sorel, Montreal or Lachine.

From Longueuil westward two sets of townships were laid out, amounting to eighteen in all. The townships were not named but numbered consecutively from east to west, each being a long, narrow strip of land stretching back from a body of water, and eventually to be incorporated into the existing seigneurial system. Townships one to eight fronting on the St. Lawrence, and known as the "Royal Townships", were allotted to Sir John Johnson's Royal Yorkers, to be divided at his request among prospective settlers according to race and religion. The first township was given to Catholic Highlanders; the second to Scottish Presbyterians; the third to German Calvinists; the fourth to German Lutherans; the fifth to Anglicans; and the sixth, seventh and eighth, those immediately to the east of Gananoque, to Major Jessup's Corps.

The "Cataraqui Townships", stretching westward from Fort Frontenac, consisted of ten townships. The first of these townships was given to Captain Grass' party from New York; the second was allotted to the remainder of Major Jessup's Corps; the third township was to be settled by Sir John Johnson's 2nd Battalion and the King's Rangers; the fourth township was allotted to Major Peter VanAlstine's party from New York; and the fifth township, later named Marysburgh, was given to a detachment of disbanded regulars including forty German mercenaries under Baron von Reitzenstein. The remaining five townships circled the Bay of Quinte, going around Picton Bay and the high shore to Green Point, and on along the bay shore to the Carrying Place. The eighth township followed the north shore of the bay, the ninth joined the land reserved for the Mohawks, and the tenth went beyond, to the land along Mohawk Bay and the Napanee River.

Camp in the forest

The Indian Loyalists

Some of the first Loyalist settlers on the Bay of Quinte were the Mohawk Indians. On May 22, 1784 a band of them under the leadership of Chiefs John Deserontyou, Aaron Hill and Isaac Hill landed with fifteen canoes near the present village of Deseronto. They had been supporters of the British during the Revolutionary War.

The conflict between white men, which had swept the North American continent, also had affected the heart of the Six Nations Confederacy in the Mohawk Valley. Rebel as well as Loyalist agents had been active among the Indians there, each trying to win them to their side. The Indians were caught in the middle. Having no cause to turn their backs on their friends and neighbours with whom they had lived for so many years, they had nothing to lose or to gain by observing neutrality. Perhaps most of them would have remained silent observers witnessing the gigantic struggle between treason and loyalty, if Joseph Brant, their great chief and a fervent Loyalist, had not made them choose sides.

Brant was thirty-three when the Revolution broke out. Through him the majority of the Six Nations Indians declared their intention to join the Loyalists. In the course of events they fought against the rebels as well as against one of their own tribes, the Oneidas, who had sided with the Revolutionaries. When Sir John Johnson fled his estate in Tryon County in 1776 to organize resistance in Canada, Brant followed him, and he was in Montreal when Ethan Allen attempted to capture that city for the rebels. Some of the Mohawks who lived near Fort Hunter went to Fort Niagara, and some settled at Lachine, near Montreal, in the fall of 1777. During the war the Indians at Fort Niagara fought under Colonel Butler, under Chief Joseph Brant, and other leaders. The Indians who had settled around Montreal, took part in the war under Captains John Deserontyou, Aaron Hill, and Isaac Hill. They all fought with varying fortunes but without regaining their former homes. When the fighting ceased in 1781, it was obvious that the Indians who had declared themselves on the British side were entitled to compensation for their losses. But

The Mohawk Church at Brantford, built in 1785 with the aid of a grant received by the Indians from King George III, was the first Protestant church in Upper Canada. It is known as St. Paul's H. M. Chapel of the Mohawks.

during the peace conference in Paris, which was conducted in haste, the British negotiators seemed to forget just how much England owed to all the Loyalists who had fought to help maintain British power. What was even more unjust, the Indians who had so bravely defended the English Crown were not at all mentioned for consideration. This unforgivable mistake, however, was corrected later and General Haldimand was instructed to make every possible gesture of goodwill to the loyal Indians, to compensate them for their sufferings.

Landings of the Mohawks on the Bay of Quinte shore

Early in 1783, General Haldimand sent Surveyor-General Holland to the Bay of Quinte to locate and survey suitable land on which the Mohawks could settle. The survey party was accompanied by Captains Brant and Deserontyou. Both were satisfied with the location, and in October of 1783, the land between the Gananoque and Trent Rivers was secured by treaty from the aboriginal occupants, the Mississauga Indians. When Brant and Deserontyou returned from the Bay of Quinte to Lachine, however, not all the Indians were pleased with the proposed new site for settlement, and some expressed the desire to be closer to the Six Nations Indians who had remained on the American side of the border. Brant immediately conveyed their wishes to Haldimand, and asked for land at the head of Lake Ontario in the Grand River valley. Captain John Deserontyou and his followers were in favour of retaining the original Cataraqui proposal.

On May 22, 1784, a meeting took place at Niagara at which Colonel John Butler negotiated with the Mississauga Indians for the purchase of land lying between Lakes Ontario, Huron and Erie. Part of this large tract of land was to be reserved for the use of the Mohawk Indians. The chief of the Mississaugas declared his people's willingness to sell the land and to accommodate their brethren of the Six Nations. Accordingly a tract of land, consisting of over half a million acres along the Grand River, was allocated to the Mohawk Indians. The new settlement which became known as "Mohawk Village" soon had about 24 houses, and a chapel was built. An historical plaque erected by the Ontario Archaeological and Historical Sites Board explains:

St. Paul's 1785, H. M. Chapel of the Mohawks. This chapel, the first Protestant church in Ontario, was built with the aid of a grant obtained by Joseph Brant from George III. It replaced the Queen Anne Chapel at Fort Hunter, N. Y., lost as a result of the Mohawk's alliance with the British during the American Revolution. Early services were conducted by Rev. Robt. Addison but the first two resident incumbents were Rev. Wm. Hough 1826 and Rev. Robt. Lugger 1827-37. It was consecrated by Bishop C. J. Stewart 1830 and named a Royal Chapel by Edward VII 1904.

Settlers drawing location tickets for their farms

The Allocation of
Land

About the middle of June 1784, the first parties of Loyalists began to arrive at different locations along the St. Lawrence River, the Bay of Quinte and at other destinations. They were followed by others who continued to disembark throughout the summer of that year. Some of the townships were not surveyed as yet, and for the time being the settlers stayed in tents supplied by the government. They were tired, but looking forward to establishing permanent homes, clearing the forest and raising their first crops, although it was too late in the season to plant anything that year. By the end of the summer the survey had progressed sufficiently to permit the allocation of land in lots.

Surprisingly, the allocation was carried out smoothly considering the primitive conditions and the extent of the work involved. Land was allotted according to status and rank. Disbanded privates were entitled to receive one hundred acres each on the river front, designated as the first concession, and two hundred acres in the second or third concessions which were considered as "remote" areas. In addition to this, fifty acres each were allotted to wives and to each of their children. Upon coming of age, each son and daughter was entitled to an additional two hundred acres. Officers' grants were considerably larger. Non-commissioned officers were to receive 200 acres; subalterns, 500; captains, 700; and field officers, 1,000. The 84th Regiment, however, pointed out that its members had been promised grants of 5,000 acres for field officers, with comparable declining grants for lesser officers; consequently, all grants to the military were raised to this level. The Loyalists were ranked with the disbanded soldiers according to their losses. The Cataraqui townships were settled predominately by disbanded soldiers and their families, although some of the settlers were Loyalists who had not served in the army.

Townships were divided into concessions, and each concession was laid out into lots of two hundred acres each, with four lots having a mile of frontage. Every two or three miles a strip forty feet wide was reserved for a crossroad. The lots were allocated by "draw." The drawing started in the summer of 1784, with the surveyor, in many cases, acting as the Land Agent. After completing the survey, he prepared numbered ballots corresponding to the lot numbers, and a time and place was arranged for the settlers to meet and draw their lots. The slips of paper (ballots) were placed in a hat and each applicant drew a number. Officers came first and drew their lots in the first concession fronting on the water. After the officers had been served, the other members of the company went through the same procedure. The number written on the ballot was the number of the applicant's lot. The surveyor at once wrote the name of the person who had drawn the number in the appropriate place on his map and gave him a certificate, or "location ticket".

In the beginning, only the first concessions of the townships were laid out. As they fronted on a body of water, they were more readily accessible to the settlers than the back concessions which could only be reached by traversing a dense trackless forest. It was not until a year or two later that the second and third concessions were surveyed and some of those lots were occupied.

With their location tickets in hand, the settlers began to move to inspect their new land which in most cases consisted of forest, thick underbrush, fallen trees and swamps. Occasionally settlers exchanged locations among themselves to be near their friends with whom they had served in the same regiment. Some of the settlers who drew land never actually saw it. They sold it, sometimes for a quart of rum, or gave it away because it was located in a "remote" area somewhere in the third or fourth concession. Others retained their lots fronting on the water and sold a lot to the rear of the township for clothing, seed grain or livestock. As a rule, the seller wrote his name on the back of his location ticket when the transfer was made. Often, after a ticket had changed hands several times, the ownership of the land became difficult to determine and the government eventually created a Land Board for each township, to examine the land claims and solve the problems that had arisen.

The Royal Townships

The Royal Townships, as they were called, consisted of nine townships, although only eight were considered suitable for settlement. No value was attached to the township of Lancaster which, being swampy, was known as the "sunken township". In 1788 the previously numbered townships were given the following names: No. 1, Lancaster; No. 2, Charlottenburgh; No. 3, Cornwall; No. 4, Osnabruck; No. 5, Williamsburgh; No. 6, Matilda; No. 7, Edwardsburgh; No. 8, Augusta; and No. 9, Elizabethtown. The townships are located on the north side of the St. Lawrence River, and comprise the counties of Glengarry, Stormont, Dundas, Grenville and part of Leeds.

Encampment of Loyalists at New Johnstown, a settlement on the St. Lawrence River, 1784, now the site of the City of Cornwall.

Prior to the arrival of the first settlers in June of 1784, the land facing the river had been partially surveyed, the work having started in 1783 and being continued in 1784 by various groups of surveyors under the direction of Major Holland. However, even before the survey had commenced, a few small settlements, mainly by squatters, had sprung up in different places along the river. One of these settlements was Cornwall, which in the early days was known as New Johnstown.

The first regular settlers in the counties of Glengarry, Stormont and Dundas were officers and men of the First Battalion of the King's Royal Regiment of New York, stationed with their wives and children at the close of the war on Isle aux Noix and Carleton Island. There were 1,462 persons who settled in the townships of Charlottenburgh, Cornwall, Osnabruck, Williamsburgh and Matilda. The men from the Royal Highland Emigrant Regiment, or the 84th, also settled in Glengarry County and vicinity.

Among the first settlers of the Royal Townships, along the St. Lawrence River, were Captain Thomas Frazer, Captain William Frazer, Lieutenant Solomon Snider, Lieutenant Gideon Adams, Captain Simon Covelle, Captain Drummond, Ensign Dulmage, Ensign Sampson, Lieutenant Farrand, Captain Amberson, Lieutenant McLean, Lieutenant James Campbell, Lieutenant Alexander Campbell, Sergeant Benoni Wiltsie, Ensign E. Bolton, Captain Justus Sherwood, Captain John Jones, and Lieutenant James Breakenridge.

The centre of the Glengarry settlement was Williamstown, named after Sir William Johnson. Here his son, Sir John Johnson, erected the first grist mill and sawmill on the Au Raisin River about 1790, and on the opposite bank he built a manor-house. To the town he gave twelve acres of land to be used as a fairground. Under the auspices of the Glengarry Agricultural Society, it became the site of Ontario's oldest continually operated fair.

The most prominent Loyalists in Glengarry were the Macdonells. Eighty-four men of the same name received land grants there, and many of them served in important positions. Lieutenant-Colonel John Macdonell (Aberchalder), a distinguished officer in the Royal Highland Emigrants (84th Regiment) and with Butler's Rangers, built a most impressive house in 1791 which was burned in 1813. He was the Speaker of the first Legislative Assembly of Upper Canada. Another noted Loyalist was Captain Samuel Anderson, who was one of the first to settle on the site of present-day Cornwall. At the outbreak of the American Revolution he was imprisoned by the rebels, having refused a commission in the Continental Army. He escaped in 1776 and was appointed a captain in the First Battalion, King's Royal Regiment of New York. He became a Justice of the Peace for the Cornwall area in 1785, and later served as the first judge of the Eastern District.

Some of the other early settlers in the Cornwall area were: James Gray, Richard Duncan, Malcolm McMartin, Richard Wilkinson, Peter Everitt, Neil McLean, Jacob Farrand, William Faulkner and Walter Sutherland.

Plaque at Williamstown, Glengarry County. Here, on the Au Raisin River, Sir John Johnson built a grist mill and a sawmill in 1790.

Settlers building their first log cabin

One of the outstanding Loyalists and personalities of the Revolutionary War was Colonel John Munro. At the time the war started, Munro had extensive land holdings in the Mohawk Valley. He was a close friend of Sir John Johnson, well educated and a successful businessman. His estate, like those of other prominent Loyalists, was confiscated. Together with Sir John Johnson, Colonel Butler and others, he escaped to Montreal, where he was appointed commanding officer of the 1st King's Royal New York Regiment. He and his regiment took part in many of the battles, fought under Carleton, Clinton, Burgoyne and Simcoe, and were involved in various skirmishes along the New York State border. After the war, Munro joined his disbanded soldiers at New Johnstown (Cornwall), where he received land grants in what is now the Township of Matilda, Dundas County. There on the river front, he built "Munro Hall", an early landmark in the area. Munro's hospitality was well known to those who travelled from Montreal to York (Toronto), and among the guests who stayed at his home were Lord Dorchester, Chief Justice Osgoode, Colonel John Butler, the Reverend John Stuart, the Reverend John Bethune, and the Reverend John Strachan. John Munro was the first to represent the County of Dundas in the first Parliament of Upper Canada.

The three townships, Edwardsburgh, Augusta and Elizabethtown, in Leeds and Grenville Counties, were allocated to Major Jessup's Corps. In the year 1784 the township of Edwardsburgh received 166 settlers, Augusta 228, and Elizabethtown 182 — a total of 576 men, women and children. Among the prominent early settlers were Dr. Solomon Jones, Major Edward Jessup and Captain Justus Sherwood. The majority of Jessup's Rangers were experienced farmers and labourers, the remainder were artisans, merchants, a few schoolmasters, two doctors and a clergyman.

Thousand Islands, St. Lawrence River

A logging scene in Upper Canada

Justus Sherwood was born in Connecticut. At the outbreak of the American Revolution, he was arrested as a Loyalist, but escaped to join the British at Crown Point. He was taken prisoner at Saratoga in 1777 and, after being exchanged, was commissioned as a captain in the intelligence service. In 1784 he took up land in Augusta Township and played a leading role in its settlement.

Other well-known Loyalists of Leeds and Grenville were Elijah Bottum, a brother-in-law of Justus Sherwood; William Buell, the founder of Brockville; Peter Drummond; Daniel Jones, brother of Dr. Solomon Jones; Ephraim Jones; and Thomas Sherwood, father of Adiel and Reuben Sherwood.

There were many Loyalists by the name of Jones who distinguished themselves during the Revolutionary War. One Jones was condemned to be hanged no less than three times in attempts to get him to divulge information on the movements of the King's forces. Three times he refused to answer questions saving his life only with his determination to remain silent. Another, Ephraim Jones, had been a resident of the Mohawk Valley. He escaped to Montreal, and his two brothers made it safely to Nova Scotia. Ephraim received 300 acres of land in the Township of Augusta.

Thomas Sherwood, who settled in Elizabethtown in 1784, is regarded as the first settler in Leeds and Grenville; he obtained lot No. 1 in the first concession. Prior to the Revolutionary War he and his two brothers, Seith and Adiel, had owned land five miles north of Fort Edward where, on October 17, 1777, General Burgoyne surrendered to General Gates. At the beginning of the war, Sherwood, who remained loyal to the British Crown, escaped, making his way via Lake Champlain to St. John, where he joined the British troops serving in Major Jessup's Corps. His son, Adiel Sherwood, who was Sheriff of Leeds and Grenville, left a description of life in the early days of Upper Canada:

After the first year, we raised a supply of Indian corn, but had no mill to grind it, and were therefore compelled to pound it in a large mortar, manufacturing what we call "samp", which was made into the Indian bread called by the Dutch "suppawn". The mortar was constructed in the following manner: We cut a log from a large tree, say two and one-half feet in diameter, and six feet in length, placed it firmly in the ground, so that about two feet projected above the surface, then carefully burned the centre of the top so as to form a considerable cavity, which was then scraped clean. We generally selected an iron-wood tree about six inches in diameter from which to make the pestle. Many a time I have pounded with one until the sweat ran merrily down my back. Although this simple contrivance did well enough for corn, it did not answer for grinding wheat. The government, seeing this difficulty, built a mill back of Kingston, where the inhabitants, for seven miles below Brockville, got their grinding done.

In our neighbourhood they got along well enough in summer by lashing two wooden canoes together. Three persons would unite to manage the craft, each taking a grist. It generally took about a week to perform the journey. After horses were procured, kind Providence furnished a road on the ice until the road was passable by land. What is wonderful is that during the past fifty years it has been practicable for horses and sleighs to traverse the ice from Brockville to Kingston, such a way having been provided only when absolutely necessary for the settlers.

Among the best known United Empire Loyalist families in the Brockville area were the Buells. From the time William Buell built his first log cabin on the site of Brockville in 1785, the family steadily rose to prominence and wealth, exercising control of public affairs in Brockville as well as Upper Canada.

At the beginning of the Revolutionary War, William Buell, loyal to the British Crown, left his property to the rebels and made his way through the wilderness to Montreal, where he joined the King's Rangers and became a lieutenant. He served in the army for seven years as quartermaster and on frequent occasions acted as a secret service agent carrying important messages from Canada to the British Commander in New York. Twice he was captured by rebels, and many a time he escaped by a hair's breadth. He was present at Saratoga at the time of General Burgoyne's surrender. In March, 1782, Buell married Martha Norton whose father was a Loyalist from Farmington, Connecticut. After the war, in 1785, they settled at the present site of the City of Brockville, at that time nothing more than a wilderness. In 1800 Buell was elected a member of the House of Assembly for Upper Canada, serving in this capacity for four years. A highly respected man in his community, he was generous in character and liberal in his politics. In the early days, Brockville was called Buell's Bay; later when a Court House was built there, it was named Elizabethtown, and eventually it was renamed Brockville in honour of General Brock. William Buell died in 1832 in his 81st year. His son, William Buell, was the proprietor of the *Brockville Gazette* for twenty-five years.

Brockville Court House, 1844. When Elizabethtown, as Brockville then was called, became the capital of the district, a frame court house was built in 1810. It was replaced by a brick structure in 1824, and twenty years later this impressive stone structure was erected.

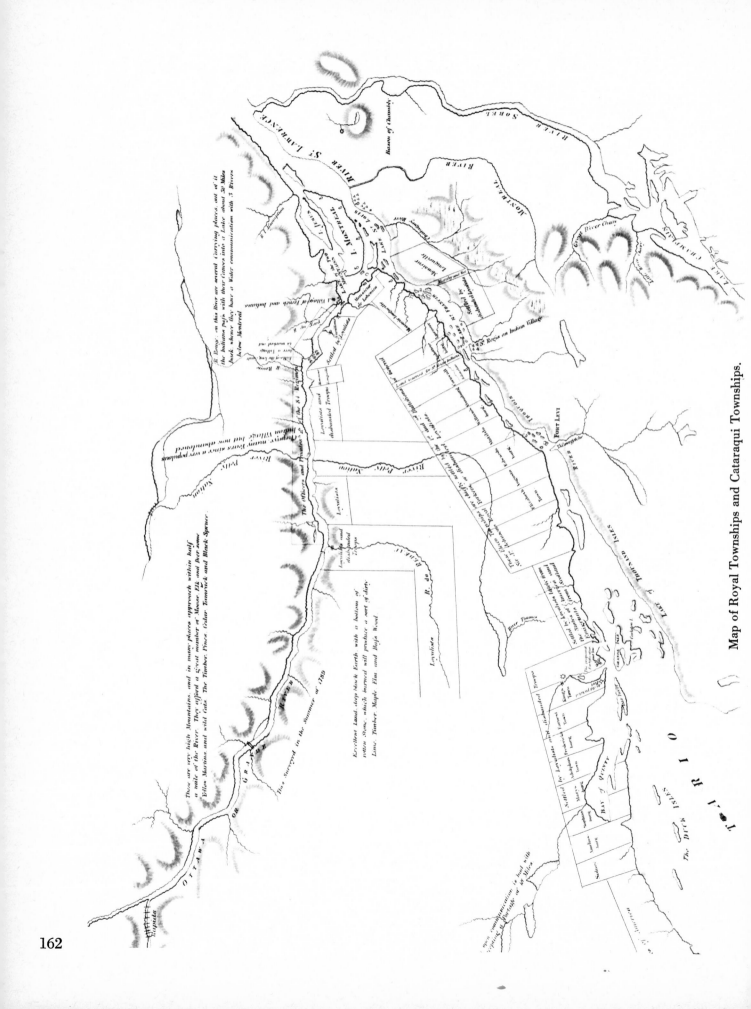

Map of Royal Townships and Cataraqui Townships.

The founder of the town of Gananoque was Joel Stone who, in 1777 took up arms against the rebels and served in the army until the evacuation of British soldiers from New York. He was born in Guildford, Connecticut, and owned extensive properties which he lost on account of his adherence to the Crown. Stone came to Canada in 1786, and in 1789 received 700 acres of land on the west bank of the Gananoque River, where he built a sawmill and a grist mill and established a mercantile business. In 1798 Joel Stone began a courtship by correspondence with the widow of Abraham Dayton who had settled in Burford Township, near Brantford. The couple was married in the summer of 1799. Later Stone obtained permission to operate a ferry across the Gananoque River, and in 1806 he formed a committee for the erection of a bridge. He was appointed a Justice of the Peace in 1800, and was a colonel in command of the 2nd Leeds Militia when United States forces raided his village in September of 1812. He died on the 20th of November, 1833.

Joel Stone (1749-1833), founder of the town of Gananoque

A plaque honours Gananoque's founder, Joel Stone. Standing in front of the plaque are from left to right: Mr. Ian Beresford, Mayor of Gananoque; Rev. R. Booth; Mr. Ronald McMurrich; Miss Louie Macdonald, great-great-granddaughter of Joel Stone; Prof. G. F. G. Stanley.

The Jessups were among the distinguished Loyalist families who, without hesitation, had declared their loyalty to the King. Colonel Edward Jessup was born in the parish of Stamford in the County of Fairfield, Connecticut, in 1735. At the beginning of the Revolutionary War he and his family resided in Albany, New York. He forfeited 500,000 acres of land by taking up arms against the American rebels. After raising a corps of volunteers, Jessup joined the British army under General Burgoyne who at the time was marching on Ticonderoga, and he continued serving in the struggle to uphold British supremacy. At the end of the war, his corps was disbanded; and its members were settled in what is now Leeds and Grenville Counties, and on the Bay of Quinte. When he had completed the location of his men, Major Jessup proceeded to England where he remained for several years to present his own claims. Concerned about the lack of beasts of burden in the new settlements of Upper Canada, he wrote from London to Governor Haldimand, proposing to have the settlers cut oak trees and make barrel staves in the winter for export to England, in order to earn money to buy oxen. His suggested scheme was not implemented, and the scarcity of cattle in Upper Canada continued for some time, slowing down progress.

A plaque honours Brockville's founder, William Buell. Standing in front of the plaque are, from left to right: Mr. Allan Buell of Ottawa, Colonel Donald B. Buell of Ottawa, and Mr. Kenneth Buell of Brockville.

A plaque honours Merrickville's founder, William Merrick. Standing in front of the plaque are from left to right: Mr. W. Harry Millar, Mr. D. Gordon Blair, Mr. J. K. Abbott, Mr. William B. Merrick, Mr. Gregory Merrick, Mr. F. M. Cass, Mr. H. Douglas Wise, Col. Duncan Douglas, and Prof. W. S. Goulding.

Jessup received no money for his losses but was given extensive land grants in the Township of Augusta, Grenville County, for his services. He selected lots Number 1, 2 and 3 in the first concession. In 1810 a town site was surveyed on his grant which he named Prescott in honour of Robert Prescott, Governor-in-Chief of Canada, 1797-1807. Jessup then built on the site a schoolhouse and a residence for a teacher. He died at Prescott in February, 1816, at the age of 81. Most of his adult life had been spent defending the Crown and trying to keep the country under the British flag. In Upper Canada he helped to carve out of the wilderness the farmland that would sustain the generations to come.

The Burritt family came from Arlington, Vermont. Two young brothers, Stephen and Adaniram, both engaged on the side of the British, took part in the Battle of Bennington, Vermont. Having been defeated, they were thrown into jail, but managed to escape and make their way to St. John, Quebec, where they again joined the British army. Having been discharged at the end of the war, Stephen drew lot No. 29 in the first concession of Augusta. He returned to St. John, where he met his father Daniel and the rest of the family whom he brought back to Augusta. Being adventurous of spirit, he went on an exploratory expedition along the Rideau River. At what is now Burritt's Rapids, he laid the groundwork for a new settlement in the Township of Marlborough. Here his son Edmund was born, the first white child on the Rideau. Stephen Burritt represented Grenville County in the House of Assembly from 1808 to 1812. He was the first postmaster of Burritt's Rapids, and during the War of 1812 he served as a lieutenant-colonel in the militia. He died at the age of 84, and was buried in Christ Church cemetery at Burritt's Rapids.

Most of the Loyalists were industrious people who, under most primitive conditions, managed to cultivate farms, build mills and establish businesses. William Merrick, a Loyalist from Massachusetts, built a mill on the Rideau River which formed the nucleus of a small community known as Merrick's Mill and later became the village of Merrickville. Abel Stevens, a Loyalist and early industrialist from Vermont, built in 1796 the first mill at Delta, Leeds County, which to this day is preserved as a fine example of early Canadian architecture and as a reminder of the pioneer industries that started the development of eastern Ontario.

Cataraqui Settlement

Kingston Township

In June, 1784, the first party of settlers under Captain Michael Grass landed at Cataraqui with men, women and children. There were 187 settlers designated for the first township at Cataraqui. In 1788, when all the townships were given names, this first township became known as Kingstown. A town plot was surveyed by Lieutenant John Frederick Holland, a son of the Surveyor-General, during the winter of 1783 and 1784. The township survey was carried out by John Collins, Deputy Surveyor-General, during the month of October, 1783. The township was settled predominantly by the Associated or Incorporated Loyalists who originally came from New England, New Jersey, Pennsylvania and Virginia. They had assembled in New York in 1783 and were incorporated into companies on the order of Sir Guy Carleton. Under the leadership of Captain Grass, they had been brought by sea to Sorel, Quebec, and the following year by bateaux to Cataraqui.

Among the many prominent persons who settled in the first township was the Reverend John Stuart, an unincorporated Loyalist, who arrived at Kingston a few months after Captain Grass had landed. Reverend Stuart was born in Pennsylvania. He was ordained in 1770 and sent to Fort Hunter, New York, as a missionary to the Mohawks. He was closely associated with the Johnson family and with Chief Joseph Brant. Compelled to leave Fort Hunter in 1781, he came to Kingstown and settled on lot 24, just west of the new town, where he was appointed chaplain to the 2nd Battalion of the King's Royal Regiment of New York. He thus became the first resident Anglican clergyman in what is now Ontario. Reverend Stuart ministered to the white and Indian settlers of this area, and visited as far west as Niagara and the Grand River. He was the first chaplain of the Legislative Council of Upper Canada, and was responsible for the building of Kingston's earliest church, St. George's, in 1792.

Among the early settlers in the first township were: Jos. Hackman, Captain Michael Grass, Reverend John Stuart, Lieutenants Ellerbeck, Galloway, Moore, Charles Grass, Captain Maguire, Lieutenant Atkinson, Robert VanAlstine, Lieutenant Louis Kotte, Captain Everett and Captain Auser, John Spiers, Ben Vancurat, Sergeant D. Purdy, John Connon, Mr. McCarty, Chris. Myers, Leo R. Graham, Richard Hall, Matthew Burnett and Captain Gale.

Loyalists landing on the Bay of Quinte shore.

Ernestown Township

The second township was named after Prince Ernest, the eighth child of King George III. It was surveyed by Deputy Surveyor-General Collins in November 1783, and comprised six square miles of land situated on the north side of Lake Ontario. It was settled in 1784 by 434 Loyalists of Jessup's Rangers.

On the shore of Lake Ontario developed the village of Bath which in the early days played a very important role in Upper Canada. The first library and grammar school in Upper Canada were opened here in 1811. The first steamship on Lake Ontario, the *Frontenac,* was built at Finkle's shipyard in Bath.

About the same time the Loyalist Trail (also called Bath Road) was established between Bath and Kingston. On this road still stands the house built by Loyalist Captain Jeptha Hawley in 1785. Captain Hawley had joined the Royal Standard in 1776 and settled in Ernestown in 1784.

In 1791 St. John's Church was erected on land donated by William Fairfield Sr. who with his wife Abigail Baker, had come to Canada in 1778. In 1793 Fairfield built a commodious house which was named "The White House". It is located on Highway 33, about ten miles west of Kingston. This house was occupied by the family for six generations and is one of the province's few remaining 18th century Loyalist residences. It was recently acquired by the government for preservation.

Among the earliest settlers of Ernestown were: Captain William Fraser, Captain Myers, Lieutenant Dusenbury, Lieutenant Bert, Corporals Charles and Shipley, David Dulmage, H. Conkright, Jeptha Hawley, Henry Davey, John Lindsay, John Conklin, Lieutenant John Robins, Sergeant Williams, Lieutenant Best, John Snider, James Huffman, Lieutenant Parrot, Moses Crankshaw, Sergeant Taylor, Robert Clark, Matthew Rose, Tim Porter, William Fairfield, Edward Frost, Captain W. Johnston, Sergeant Washburn, Asa Hough, Peter VanAlstine, Cris Abram, Corporals Switzer and Finkle, Jake Hesse, Peter Daly, Tim Poste, James Amers, Martin Hover, Russell Pitman and Dan Kerr, John Asselstine, Solomon Ball, Joshua Booth, Thomas Fraser, Jacob Hoffman, Andrew Miller, William Perry, Daniel Rose, and Marcus Snyder.

St. John's Church at Bath, erected 1791.

The White House, built in 1793 by Loyalist William Fairfield, Sr., is located on Highway 33, west of Kingston.

Fredericksburgh Township

The third township, Fredericksburgh, was named in 1788 after Frederick, Duke of Sussex, the ninth child of King George III. The first survey of this township was made in 1783. The original settlers of the township were Loyalists of Sir John Johnson's King's Royal Regiment of New York, and Major Robert Rogers' company, consisting of 539 settlers.

Some of the original settlers were: Thomas Bell, Peter Bowen, Edward Carscallen, John Cornelius, John Dafoe, Jacob Diamond, Jacob Ferguson, Adam Hedlor, Henry Loucks, John Mills, Jacob Pattingall, Timothy Prindle, Zenus Ross, Captain T. Anderson, Sergeant Annesley, Richard Albury, William Bell, Elijah Barclay, Ashel Bradshaw, Abram Barber, Jacob Birch, Sergeant Alex. Clark, Corporal Christy, Captain Crawford, Lemuel Caswall, Sergeant Cobham, Hugh Campbell, John Collins, Garrett Dingman, John Dinand, Adjutant Fraser, Moses Foster, T. Ferguson, Corporal Fairchild, T. Terrington, Ben. Green, John Gardiner, Lieutenant J. Howard, Thomas Howard, Sergeant Hurd, Nathan Harris, John Hunter, John Jones, Joe Kemp, Dan Lambert, S. Law, Sergeant Murdoff, Lieutenant McCoy, J. W. Taggart, K. McPherson, John McArthur, Joe Marsh, Thomas Moreland, Allan McDonnell, Sergeant Nicholson, Seth Phillips, William Pringle, George Patterson, Dave Palmer, Michael Reid, Thomas Radford, W. Shaw, John Bleecker, John Climes, Jacob Cooms, Corporal Clock, Matthew Dibs, M. Ryckman, P. Dogstrader, Valentine Detlor, G. Finkle, Peter Fike, John Grout, Abram Gravenstein, Jacob Duffman, Bruyn Huff, Phil Huffman, Joel Hough, James Keller, William VanKoughnet, John Reister, Corporal Rombough, George Roll, Tobias Stealey, Fred. Swartzeger, Luke Snider, Sergeant Scrambling, Lieutenant Swarmahorn, Jonas and Tobias VanAlstine, Rudolf Vandicor, Sergeant D. Vanderheiden, Sergeant J. Weager, John Weister, Alse. Woodcock, Sergeant Hercules Clark, John and Luke Carscallen, Captain Gummersall, Lieutenant W. McKay, Major James Rogers, Lieutenants Richard and Robertson.

Adolphustown

The fourth township, Adolphustown, was named after Adolphus, Duke of Cambridge, tenth son of George III. The lots in this township were granted to Loyalists of DeLancey's Corps. A party of some 250 of these Loyalists under Major Peter VanAlstine landed on June 16, 1784, from bateaux near the present village of Adolphustown. They had sailed from New York to escape persecution by the rebels.

VanAlstine was of Dutch ancestry. He was appointed justice of the peace and represented this area in the first Legislative Assembly of Upper Canada. At Glenora he built the earliest grist mill in Prince Edward County.

The township was surveyed in November 1783. During the drought years of 1787 and 1788 many of the early settlers were near starvation. They were forced to sell their land to merchants for food. Later this land was resold to new immigrants.

On March 6, 1792, the community held its first town meeting, with Ruben Bedell as the first town clerk. The present church of St. Alban-the-Martyr, erected between 1884 and 1888, at Adolphustown, was built by public subscription as a memorial to the Loyalists of the area. On June 16, 1884 a monument was erected at the edge of the old burial ground to commemorate the centennial celebration of the landing of the Loyalists. In June 1958, a park was opened along the shore of the Bay. It includes the burial ground of the early settlers and a Loyalist Museum.

Among the early settlers were: Lieutenant Vandervort, Major VanAlstine, James Schwarmahorn, Isaac Young, C. Petersen, John Baker, J. Hoover, Lieutenant Rustin, J. Fitzgerald, J. Elleson, Conrad Vandusen, J. Rusk, Joe. Hofnagle, Captain Maybee, John Hartman, Lieutenant Paul Trompour, Lieutenant Phillip Dorland, John German, C. Driskle, Moses Dean, Tobias

Ryckman, John Whitley, George Ruttan, James Thomas, Lieutenant Ben Clinch, Lieutenant S. Tuffer, Gilbert Bogart, Cornelius Van Horne, John Sharp, Lieutenant Vanord, James McMasters, Edward Staples, Nicholas Hagerman, Lieutenant T. Huyck, Paul Huff, William Clark, Albert Connell, Alex. Campbell, John Crusdel, Peter VanSkiver, Velleau, Coles, Sherman, Ballis, Thomas Dorland, William Baker, Owen Roblin, Fitzgerald, Michael Stout, Captain Joseph Allan, Hover, George Rutledge, and James Noxen.

Plaque outside the Loyalist Burying Ground, Adolphustown

Entrance to the Loyalist Burying Ground, Adolphustown

171

Present-day view of the site at Adolphustown where the Loyalists landed in 1784.

Memorial to the United Empire Loyalists, Adolphustown

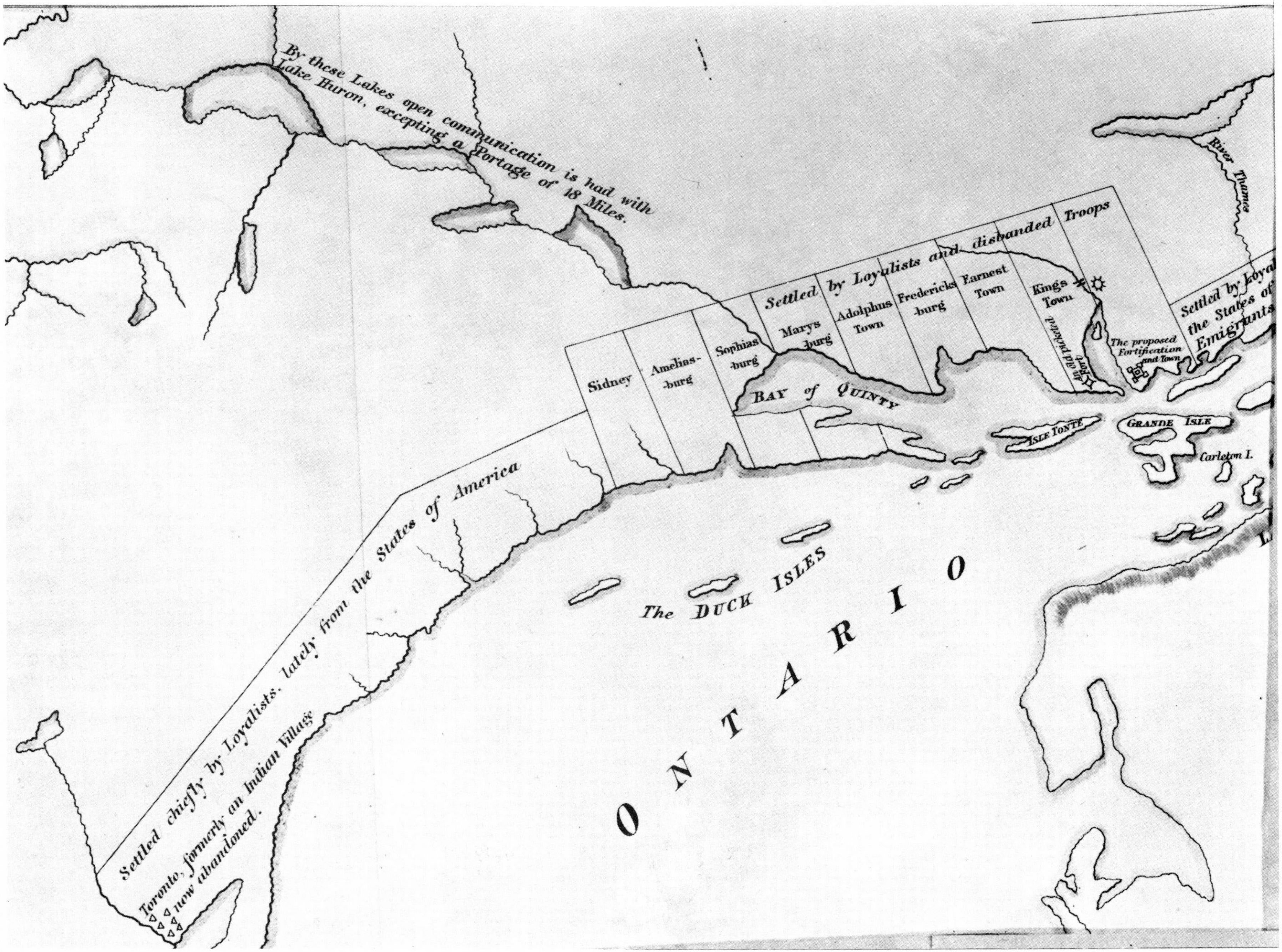

Map of the Cataraqui Townships

River Thames

Settled by Loyalists on the States of the Emigrants

The proposed Fortification and Town

An Old Fort

Kings Town

Earnest Town

Fredericks burg

Adolphus Town

Marys burg

Sophias burg

Amelias burg

Sidney

Settled by Loyalists and disbanded Troops

BAY of QUINTY

GRANDE ISLE

Tanlæm. I.

ISLE TONTE

O N T A R I O

The DUCK ISLES

States of America

By these Lakes open communication is had with Lake Huron, excepting a Portage of 18 Miles.

Settled chiefly by Loyalists, lately from the States of the States

Toronto, formerly an Indian village, now abandoned.

Marysburgh Township

This township is located on the most eastern tip of Prince Edward County. It was surveyed in 1784 by Deputy Surveyor-General John Collins. Early settlers were mostly German, Irish and English soldiers taking up their land grants following the American Revolution. Few had farming experience and many suffered great hardships in the early days. Their leader was Colonel Archibald Macdonnell, who was related to Bishop Macdonnell of Kingston.

Among the settlers was a small group of disbanded German mercenaries under Baron von Reitzenstein. By October, 1784, this party, numbering about forty persons, had settled in Marysburgh township and begun to clear and cultivate the land. Shortly after, they erected a log chapel just west of what is now the North Marysburgh Museum. They were ministered to by a Lutheran missionary. This was one of the earliest German-speaking groups to settle in Ontario.

The Lutheran congregation eventually dwindled in numbers and the log chapel was abandoned. Peter Rose, a Loyalist on whose property the church was built, tore it down and from the squared timbers erected the framework for his new house. This home remained in the Rose family for six generations. It is now owned by the Township of North Marysburgh and houses the North Marysburgh Museum. Directly in front of the museum, near the shore, is the "Old Dutch Burying Ground" or Rose Cemetery, as it is now called. Here are buried most of the first settlers of the Hessian Regiment, among other pioneers.

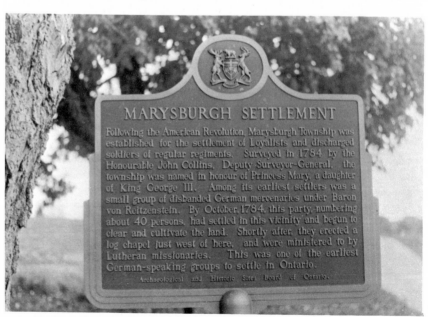

Plaque on the grounds of the North Marysburgh Museum

Marysburgh was the first township to be settled in Prince Edward County. Among the early settlers were: Lieutenant Moor Hoventon, R. Ferguson, D. Cole, Captain Ruttan, Matthew Benson, T. Goldsmith, German, Vandusen, Inglehart, Lieutenant Thompson, Major James Rogers, Lieutenants Church and Spencer, and Lieutenant Young and his brother. Also Alex Carney, William Carson, James and Peter Clarke, Peter Collier, Henry Davis, Samuel Farington, Frederick Fisher, James and Thomas Grant, William and Walter Ross, Henry Smith and Daniel Wright.

The *Rose House*, now the North Marysburgh Museum, was built before 1820.

Sophiasburgh Township

The township was surveyed in 1785 by Louis Kotte. Settlement, however, commenced around 1777 or 1778 when squatters who came from New York State took up land near the head of Picton Bay. Proper settlement began at Picton Bay in 1787 when two Congers, Peterson, Spencer, Henry Jackson and later Barker and Vandusen obtained land.

The great bulk of land around the waterfront has been "located" by United Empire Loyalists of Fredericksburgh and Adolphustown who "drew" it under Governor Simcoe's proclamation, but having already established themselves, they held this land without settling on it and sold it when the opportunity presented itself.

Many of the first actual settlers in this township were so-called "Late Loyalists". These were American colonists who, although they had sympathized with the British, were not driven from their homes by the rebels as many others had been, but they were either dissatisfied with the new order of things after the return of peace, or what was more likely, induced by the Proclamation of Governor Simcoe, they followed in the steps of the original Loyalists.

Some of the settlers of Sophiasburgh had first lived in Adolphustown. Stephen Conger, a Loyalist from New Jersey who settled in this township in 1787, donated land and material for a church which was built by William Moore and financed by local subscription. Known as "The White Chapel", it was the first Methodist church in Prince Edward County and one of the earliest in Upper Canada. It has been maintained as a place of worship for a longer period than any other church of Methodist origin in Ontario. Other early settlers in this township included: John and Owen Ritchie, Phillip Roblin, Ryckman, Dean Trompour, and Hagerman.

The White Chapel, near Picton, Ontario, was the first Methodist church built in Prince Edward County.

Ameliasburgh

The "Seventh Town" of Upper Canada is the last of the three original townships of Prince Edward County. The survey started in 1785, but Ameliasburgh was settled even before the survey commenced.

John Weese is regarded as the first settler of this township. He was an American colonist of German extraction from Herkimer County, New York. As a Loyalist he was serving two years in the British army during the Revolutionary War. He settled with his family on lot 89, concession 1 in the autumn of 1783. Another early settler was Thomas Dempsey, whose father was private secretary to General Schuyler of Hackensack, New York. Thomas Dempsey joined the Royal troops and at the end of the war fled to Canada. When the township was organized as a municipality Dempsey became the first assessor.

Elijah Wallbridge, a Loyalist from Vermont, was the first settler in the extreme eastern part of the township. He drew and also purchased large tracts of land at Mississauga Point where, still to this day, land is in the possession of his descendants. Solomon Huff, also an United Empire Loyalist, settled on the only island in Ameliasburgh, Huff's Island, about 1825.

Other early settlers were: Elias Alley, John Bleeker, John Babcock, William Anderson, the Ways, Mordens, Redners, DeLongs, Roblins, Parliaments, Spragues, Bonters, Sagers, Pecks, Onderdonks, Philip Pember, Jacob Wormley, Henry Brout, Asa Richardson, Bolton Evans, and Zenas Ross.

First settlement in the wilderness

Sidney

The eighth township, Sidney, was named after Lord Sidney who, at the time of the Revolutionary War, was Colonial Secretary. It was surveyed and laid out around 1787 by Louis Kotte, assisted by a Mr. McDonald.

Settlement was not instantaneous as it had been in townships one to five. Sidney was settled mainly by individuals who may be divided into several groups. First, there were the United Empire Loyalists; secondly, the sons and daughters of the Loyalists who had drawn land in the older townships on the Bay of Quinte; thirdly, people of Loyalist origin who came from Nova Scotia, New Brunswick and other places where they had first settled; fourthly, Americans who came after the War of 1812 or at an earlier period, and immigrants who came directly from England and bought land in the township from the government or from other settlers.

The first settlers most likely came before the survey commenced, and squatted by the Bay shore. One of the first inhabitants of Sidney was Captain John Walden Meyers who, in 1784, along with others, squatted on the front of Sidney. Meyers built a mill just east of Trenton. Having difficulties with the water supply, he moved to the banks of the Moira where he constructed a dam and erected a log grist and sawmill on the east bank of the river. In 1791 it was rebuilt of stone, and this mill is still preserved by historically-minded people of Belleville.

Captain Meyers was of German descent, and came from the vicinity of Albany on the Hudson in New York State. During the American Revolution he was a captain in the Loyal Rangers (Jessup's Corps). Immediately following the war, he settled in the Richelieu Valley and then moved to Sidney Township. During the war he displayed great bravery on the British side, and was feared by the rebels because of his bold night raids.

Among the early settlers on the first concession were Captain March, Captain John W. Meyers and his four sons, John Scott, George Smith, Abel Gilbert, the Chrysdales and the Ostroms. Later came the Zwicks, Vandervoorts, Whites, Bonesteels, Simmons', Kelly's, Finkles, Grahams, Jones', Laurences and Elijah Ketcheson. Alexander Chisholm established himself on lot 3 of concession 1 and 2 (now western Belleville). Captain George Singleton settled on lot 5 and 6, and opened a fur trading post on the east bank of the Moira River in partnership with his brother-in-law Lieutenant Isaac Ferguson. When they arrived the river was called Sagonaska by the Indians, but within a short time it became known as Singleton's Creek. When Captain Meyers built his mill there, this locality became known as Meyers' Creek. In 1816 it was renamed Belleville in honour of Arabella, the wife of Lieutenant-Governor Francis Gore.

Loyalist monument at Belleville, Ontario

Maple sugar making in the bush.

Lumber mill

Thurlow Township

The ninth town on the Bay of Quinte was surveyed in 1787 by Louis Kotte, and was named after Baron Edward A. Thurlow, an outstanding British statesman and supporter of George III. Before the survey was finished, some of the early Loyalist settlers took up land along the Moira River. During the year of 1789, Thurlow received a group of some fifty Loyalists who came from Prince Edward County. Among these arrivals, who settled some distance back from the front in the area of Foxboro, were John Taylor, William Reed, Solomon Hazelton, Archibald McKenzie, Zadock Thrasher, Richard Smith, John and Conrad Frederick and Stephen and Laurence Badgley. These were followed a few years afterwards by the families of Richard Canniff and Robert Thompson.

The names of Edward and J. Carscallion, Fairman, Bidwell, William Johnson, Samuel Sherwood, Crawford and others are inscribed on an old map of Thurlow on file in the Crown Lands office, as having settled about 1792-3 on the front of the first concession. The rear concessions were rapidly taken later on by the offspring of the United Empire Loyalists who had settled on other portions of the Bay shore. Prior to 1798 the townships of Thurlow and Sidney were united for municipal purposes. On March 5, 1798 Thurlow was allowed to have its own town meetings. Captain John McIntosh was elected as clerk; John Chisholm and William Reed were assessors, John Taylor was pound-keeper and John Fairman, constable.

The River Moira, with its many mills and manufacturing establishments in the early days, added materially to the development and wealth of Thurlow Township.

Richmond

The tenth and last town of the Cataraqui Townships was named Richmond after the Duke of Richmond. It was surveyed late in 1785, or early in the spring of 1786. At the Appanee Falls on the river which empties in the Mohawk Bay, a flouring mill was erected. This of course, attracted settlers and a small village sprang up on the south shore which was named Appanee, meaning in the Mississauga language "flour". Later the name was changed to Napanee.

Some Loyalists who had originally settled in Fredericksburgh Township, took up land on the north shore of Mohawk Bay on the Napanee River. Among them were Alexander Nicholson, Woodcock, Peterson, Campbell, Richardson, and Detlor.

Mill on the Appanee River (Napanee River), 1795.

Bush road

Bush farm

The Western

Settlements

Among the Loyalist settlements, the Western settlements which included Niagara, Essex and Long Point (Norfolk), played an important role in the early history of Upper Canada. Many of the Loyalists streaming out of the Mohawk Valley used Niagara as the gateway into Upper Canada, and a great number of them remained in the peninsula or went westward or eastward from there to found new communities.

After the French and Indian War, the British government had established a military station on the east bank of the river at Niagara to protect the flow of supplies from the St. Lawrence to the remote forts on the Upper Great Lakes. Sir William Johnson, administrator of Indian affairs, had successfully negotiated a treaty with the Senecas and the Mississaugas in August of 1764 whereby the Indians ceded to King George III a strip of land on the west side of the Niagara River between Lake Erie and Lake Ontario, four miles in width, to be used exclusively for military purposes. In the same year, a dashing young engineer of the British army, Captain John Montressor, built the first Fort Erie and a series of eleven blockhouses along the Niagara River.

During the Revolutionary War Fort Niagara was a busy post, as several regiments of the British regulars as well as Butler's Rangers and a great many Indians were stationed there. From this point originated numerous raids staged by Colonel Butler and his Indian warriors, who penetrated deep into New York state to punish the rebels for harassing Loyalists, or to rescue British subjects who wanted to leave and settle in Canada. How disturbing these punitive raids were to the rebels, became evident when Washington dispatched General Sullivan to the Niagara frontier with nearly five thousand soldiers to break the Indian Confederacy. Sullivan's army began its march through Iroquois country in 1779, systematically destroying every Indian village and forcing thousands of Indians, warriors, women and children, to flee and seek protection at Fort Niagara. During the winter of 1779-80 at Niagara, nearly four thousand Indians died from disease or starvation. To alleviate the food shortage at the fort, General

Haldimand suggested the raising of grain and livestock at Niagara and Detroit. Colonel Bolton, commanding officer at Niagara, however, pointed out in a letter to Haldimand that the Indian Treaty of 1764 expressly forbade any "improvements" at Niagara that went beyond military installations. When the influx of Loyalist refugees accelerated drastically in 1780, General Haldimand informed Bolton that it was his intention to purchase the land previously ceded by the Indians, and to have it divided into lots to be given to Loyalists who wished to cultivate the land. It was not customary for the British government in North America to permit settlement by whites on land belonging to the Indians. However, a governor would from time to time purchase a tract of land by special treaty, particularly after 1783, when land was desperately needed for the settlement of Loyalists arriving in great numbers from the rebellious colonies.

Indians seated around fire

Indian hunter and squaw

Settlement at Niagara began on the west side of the Niagara River, opposite Fort Niagara. In 1782 there were sixteen families living there, who had cleared some land and were cultivating grain, potatoes and corn. They were supplied by the government with horses, cows and hogs. The settlement increased rapidly in numbers when, in the spring of 1784, Butler's Rangers were disbanded and other Loyalists started to arrive from New York and Pennsylvania. The land obtained from the Indians had already been divided among earlier Loyalist arrivals, and the need for the purchase of additional land became a pressing matter. Consequently, a meeting was arranged at Niagara between the Mississauga Indians under Chief Pohquan, and Colonel John Butler and other British officials, to negotiate the purchase of land lying between Lake Ontario, Lake Huron and Lake Erie for the purpose of resettling His Majesty's faithful Mohawk Indians. These Indians had assisted in the Revolutionary War, and were now camped at Lachine near Montreal. The main reason, however, for obtaining more land was the government's commitment to the thousands of Loyalists who, at the end of the war, streamed into Upper Canada.

Colonel John Butler (1728-1796) raised a corps of Loyalist refugees, known as Butler's Rangers. This unit took part in many of the campaigns of the Revolutionary War. At the end of the war Colonel Butler was active in the establishment of a Loyalist settlement in the Niagara area.

The majority of the first settlers in the Niagara region were disbanded Rangers and their families, consisting of 770 men, women and children. Most, if not all, were Protestants by faith, either Anglicans, German Lutherans or Dutch Calvinists. As the survey of land had not yet progressed sufficiently by 1784, many of the settlers, waiting for their location tickets, stayed in barracks built by Colonel Butler's men during the fall and winter of 1778-79 at the site of Fort George. A full-scale survey of the Niagara settlement began in 1787 and was completed in 1789, establishing a block of eight townships: Stamford, Niagara, Grantham, Louth, Clinton, Grimsby, Saltfleet and Barton.

One of the first permanent settlements in the Niagara district was on the site of the present-day town of Niagara-on-the-Lake. It was settled by Butler's Rangers and other Loyalists arriving in the 1780's. The place was known by a variety of names, among them Butlersburg, West Niagara, and Newark. Here, at Newark, the first five sessions of Upper Canada's Legislature were held under Lieutenant-Governor Simcoe between September 17, 1792 and June 3, 1796. On the outskirts of the town lies the oldest burying ground in Ontario where, among other early Loyalist settlers, Colonel John Butler is buried. Butler was born in New London, Connecticut, and he settled in the Mohawk Valley, New York, prior to the Revolutionary War. At the outbreak of the Revolution he was compelled to leave his estate; he was assigned to Fort Niagara where, in 1777, he raised his famous corps of Loyalist refugees, known as "Butler's Rangers". This unit took an active part in many of the forays into rebel territory, and in one of them Butler's son, Walter, was killed. When his Rangers were disbanded, Colonel Butler led them to the west side of the Niagara River, and most of them settled along the river or in other parts of the Niagara peninsula. He built his own house at Niagara-on-the-Lake in 1783. Located on Mississauga Street, it is now the oldest house in the district.

A Butler's Ranger

Butler's Burying Ground, Niagara-on-the-Lake

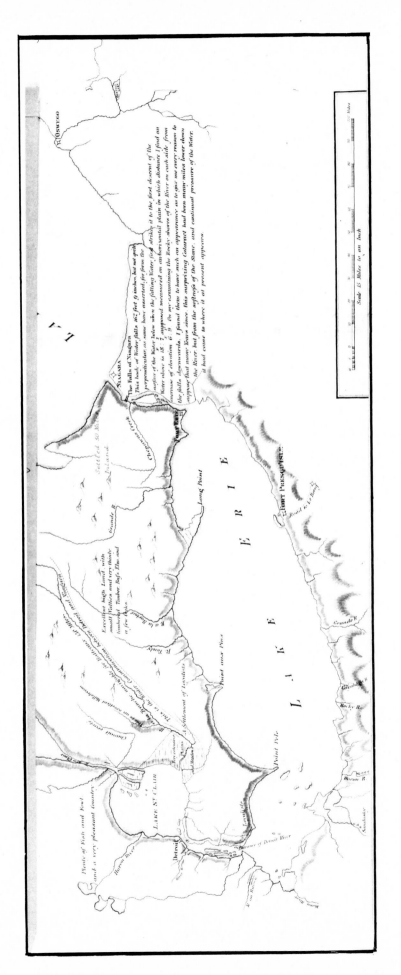

Map of the Western Settlements

Another landmark of the pioneer days at Niagara-on-the-Lake is Navy Hall. Standing on the east side of town, it was built between 1775 and 1787 for the use of officers of the Navy Department serving on Lake Ontario. During 1792 the first Parliament of Upper Canada held some of its meetings here. In 1911 the building was used as a military camp, and after restoration it became a military museum.

Many of the early settlers in the Niagara district were officers who had taken part in the Rangers' raids throughout the war. Among them were Captain Andrew Brant, Captain B. Fry, Captain P. Hare, Captain Thomas Butler, Captain Aaron Brant, Captain P. Paulding, Captain John Ball, Captain P. Ball, Captain P. Ten Brock, Lieutenant R. Clench, Lieutenant William Brant, Lieutenant William Tweeny, Lieutenant Jocal Swoos, Lieutenant James Clements, and Lieutenant D. Swoos. There were also Captain James Brant, Indian Department; Captain H. Nelles, Captain James ·Young, Captain Robert Nelles, Captain Joseph Dockater, Captain C. Ryman, Lieutenant J. Clement, Lieutenant W. B. Shuhm, Lieutenant A. Chrysler, Lieutenant S. Secord, Lieutenant F. Stevens, Surgeon R. Kerr, and Commodore T. Merritt, father of the Honourable W. H. Merritt.

Not all of the settlers concentrated along the Niagara River. Henry Nelles and two of his sons settled at Grimsby in the 1780's, as did John Green who followed shortly afterwards. They were soon joined by forty-six other families, forty-two from New Jersey and four from Pennsylvania. Among them were Andrew Pettit, John Pettit, Levi Lewis, Jacob Glover, two John Smiths, Elijah Chambers, Esea Chambers, Absol Wilcox, Allen Nixon and John Beamer.

Frederick Berger, a German soldier of the 34th Regiment who was discharged at his own request, settled in the summer of 1784 near the mouth of Frenchman's Creek, north of Fort Erie. He was the first to take up land in this area. He was soon followed by Cornelius Bowen, John Carl, John Garner, Lewis Maybee, Henry Putman, Christian Riselay, Henry Windecker, Abraham Wintermute, Benjamin Wintermute, John Wintermute, Peter Wintermute and Philip Wintermute, all of them discharged soldiers.

Thomas Merritt, a Loyalist who had served under Colonel Simcoe during the Revolutionary War, had first gone to New Brunswick, but in 1796 came to Upper Canada, landing at Queenston which at the time was an important commercial centre. Robert Hamilton, a prominent merchant, is considered the founder of the village of Queenston. The inhabitants at the time included a Mr. Crooks, a Mr. Adams and a number of Scottish merchants. Thomas Merritt soon moved on, and settled in the vicinity of present-day St. Catharines. Here he cleared the land and became a farmer. His son, William H. Merritt, was a successful merchant and mill owner. It was he who was primarily responsible for the construction of the first Welland Canal built in 1824-29.

Thomas Merritt (1759-1842) served as an officer in the Queen's Rangers during the Revolutionary War. In 1783 he settled in New Brunswick, but a few years later he moved to the Niagara peninsula where he and his family were to play a prominent role.

* * *

The original settlers of Norfolk County were nearly all United Empire Loyalists. They did not take up their land as early as did the pioneer settlers around the Bay of Quinte or in the Niagara peninsula, because most of the people who came to the Long Point (Norfolk) area had first settled in New Brunswick. Their second migration, in search of better land, was stimulated by Lieutenant-Governor Simcoe's appeal for settlers to come to Upper Canada. Simcoe, who arrived at Niagara in 1792, offered land to new settlers, particularly Loyalists and people who wished to emigrate from the United States and give their allegiance to the Crown. He believed that many of those who had remained in the United States at the close of the Revolutionary War, were now finding that the new government there was not living up to their expectations, and consequently that they could very well make good and loyal citizens of Upper Canada.

For the Loyalist settlers who came to Norfolk from New Brunswick it was a tedious and dangerous journey, travelling through dense forest and bush following the trails of the Indians. Those families who had decided to use the frail bateaux in deep water were in even greater danger, not only of losing their scant possessions but also of losing their lives. Their journey to Norfolk County in Upper Canada was no less fraught with hardship and anxieties than their expedition to New Brunswick had been, when they had first settled on the St. John River. On the grounds of South Walsingham's township office there is an historical plaque which in a nutshell explains the "Long Point Settlement":

Long Point was known to traders and travellers before the area was purchased from the Mississauga Indians in 1784. In this unsurveyed area twenty to thirty "squatters" had settled by 1791, some of whom were allowed to remain following surveys and Governor Simcoe's visit in 1795. Further land grants were made to approved applicants including many Loyalists.

Potash making in Upper Canada

The Nelles Manor at Grimsby

Among the first Loyalists who settled at Long Point, were Frederick Mabee, Peter Secord, and Peter Teeple. They arrived in 1793. Another early settler was William Smith, whose father, Abraham Smith, first came to Fort Erie by way of New Brunswick and in 1793 settled in the Young's Creek Valley in the township of Charlotteville. Jabez Culver, who came in 1794, established the first Presbyterian church in Norfolk. Thomas Welch settled in Charlotteville that year, and Edward McMichael took up land in Walsingham. In the following year came Solomon Austin, Timothy Culver and Samuel Ryerse, founder of Port Ryerse.

During the Revolutionary War, Lieutenant-Colonel Samuel Ryerse had been commissioned in the 4th New Jersey Volunteers, and after the war, like many other Loyalists, he had gone to New Brunswick. In 1794 he came to Upper Canada, and the following year he received 3,000 acres of land in Woodhouse and Charlotteville townships. At the mouth of Young's Creek he built a grist mill, around which grew the community of Port Ryerse.

Soon more Loyalists followed the trail of the first pioneers to Norfolk County. Among them were: Captain Walter Anderson, Albert Berdan, Mathias and Henry Buchner, Thomas Bowlby, Samuel Brown, William Cope, Thomas Davis, Anthony Daugherty, Daniel Freeman, Titus Finch, Elias Foster, Peter Fairchild, Reuben Green, Jacob Glover, Isaac Gilbert, Captain William Hutchinson, Daniel Hazen, John Haviland, Lawrence Johnson, Lieutenant James Munro, Peter Montross, Daniel Millard, James Matthews, Donald McCall, Abraham Powell, Joseph Ryerson, Hart Smith, William Spurgin, Silas Secord, Michael Shaw, Lot Tisdale, Jonathan Williams, Peter Wycoff, Jacob Wilson and Joseph Wilson.

Plaque commemorating Lieutenant-Colonel Samuel Ryerse

Among the early Loyalists' children who were born in Norfolk County, perhaps the best known name is that of Egerton Ryerson, founder of Ontario's school system. His father, Colonel Joseph Ryerson, distinguished himself during the Revolutionary War, taking part in many battles. After the war, Colonel Ryerson went to New Brunswick, where he married Mehetabel Stickney. His brother, Colonel Samuel Ryerson, left New Brunswick in 1794 for Norfolk County, where he settled at the mouth of Young's Creek. Joseph and his family followed him five years later. Young Egerton, who was born in Charlotteville (Turkey Point) in 1803, attended the nearby District Grammar School in Vittoria. Strongly influenced by the Methodist Society, he entered the Methodist ministry at the age of twenty-two, a fact that created friction between him and his father, who was a staunch Anglican. Egerton Ryerson's name became known for his celebrated discussions and his writings about the Clergy Reserve controversy. As the editor of the *Christian Guardian*, he defended the Methodist principles and institutions. In 1844 he was named Superintendent of Education for Upper Canada, and for the next thirty-two years he devoted his time to building up the educational system in Ontario.

When Governor Simcoe visited Norfolk County in 1795, he was so impressed with Turkey Point that he selected it as the site for a new town as well as a fort and naval station. The military post was known as Fort Norfolk, and the town, named Charlotteville, for fourteen years was the capital of the London District, organized in 1800. The fortification of Turkey Point proved to be justified during the War of 1812-14, when British soldiers were stationed here. To honour the first Lieutenant-Governor of Upper Canada, in 1829 the people of Norfolk renamed the village of Birdtown (formerly known as Theresaville) on the Lynn River as "Simcoe", now a thriving, beautiful town.

* * *

The oldest permanent settlement in Upper Canada began on the east side of the Detroit River, as a fur trading post, during the period of French rule. The post took on greater significance when, in 1734, numerous land grants were made to prospective French settlers. At the time of the British conquest of Canada, there were several hundred settlers scattered along the Detroit River; but for nearly twenty years thereafter hardly any British settlers were to be found in this area, except for a few fur traders who had come to trade with local Indians.

The American Revolution with its resulting influx of United Empire Loyalists and the King's generous land rewards for their patriotism, changed the settlements along the Detroit River almost overnight. The first to take advantage of the free land allotments in the present County of Essex were Captains Matthew Elliott and William Caldwell, who in 1783 each took up a tract of land — Elliott opposite Bois Blanc Island, and Caldwell on the site of the present town of Amherstburg. Captain William Caldwell had served during the war with Butler's Rangers, at Niagara and Detroit. After obtaining his land grant, he managed to gain control of some 11,000 additional acres on the north shore of Lake Erie, where he encouraged former Loyalist soldiers to settle. During the War of 1812 he commanded the Western Rangers in actions in Ohio, and later led the Indian forces at the battles of Chippawa, Lundy's Lane and Fort Erie. Captain Matthew Elliott came to the American colonies in 1761, and during the Revolution he served with the British forces in the Indian Department. He was an Indian agent for the western tribes from 1790 to 1795 and became deputy superintendent of the Indian Department. During the War of 1812 he took part in the capture of Detroit.

All through the Revolutionary War and for some time after the signing of the peace treaty Detroit, with its 2,500 inhabitants, remained under British control. In 1796 it was handed over, under the terms of Jay's Treaty, to the Americans. Immediately following the evacuation of the British military post at Detroit, a new establishment, known as Fort Malden, sprang up opposite Bois Blanc Island on the site of Amherstburg. This fortification was built in 1797-99 by the Second Battalion Royal Canadian Volunteers under Captain Hector MacLean. At the Amherstburg Navy Yard were built the King's ships: *Maria, Hope, Earl Camden, General Hunter, Queen Charlotte, Lady Provost, Chippawa, Little Belt* and *Detroit.* Amherstburg was strengthened during the War of 1812, and the naval force enabled the army to retain control on the western frontier.

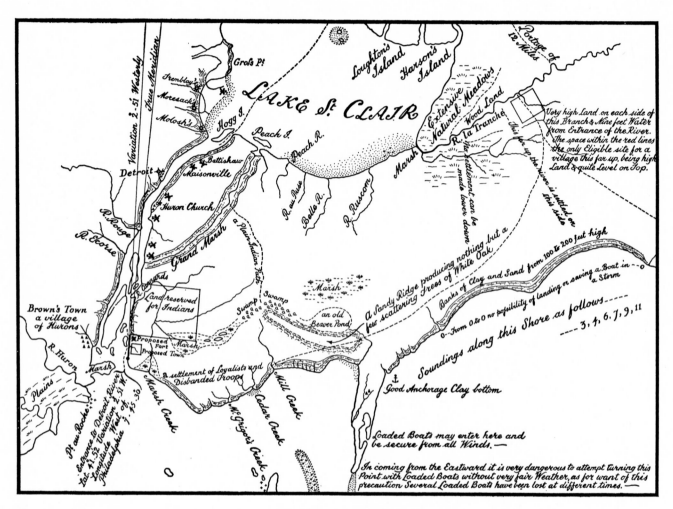

Map of Detroit River, 1791

When Detroit was transferred to the United States, two blockhouses were built on Bois Blanc Island. In the meantime, the majority of Detroit's inhabitants preferred to be on the British side, and almost two thousand of the residents moved across the river, where they founded the community of Sandwich, known in the early days as the Parish of L'Assomption. The first Anglican services were conducted there by Richard Pellard, sheriff of the Western District. In 1802 he was ordained a deacon and appointed missionary to the settlement. A log church was erected in 1807. Some of the settlers who came from Detroit, took up land near Lake St. Clair or along the Thames River. Among the newcomers was John Askin, a wealthy merchant, whose grandson, Major John Richardson, achieved fame as a Canadian writer.

Among the names of the earliest settlers of Essex County, who drew their land grants from the French Crown, were: Baby, Dumouchelle, Goyeau, Jannesse, Langlois, Marentette, Meloche and Ouellette. The Baby family achieved great prominence in the affairs of the western frontier. One of them, Jacques Baby, was appointed in 1792 to the Executive and Legislative Councils of Upper Canada. In 1807 he built the first brick house, which is still standing in Windsor.

Northeast of Windsor, at Chatham in Kent County, Lieutenant-Governor John Graves Simcoe built a blockhouse, planning to establish a small naval arsenal which would form a link in the defences of Upper Canada's western frontier and at the same time draw the Indian trade from Detroit. The post was garrisoned by a detachment of the Queen's Rangers, but was abandoned by 1797. The blockhouse was then moved to Sandwich to serve as the Western District's court house and gaol.

The early settlers in the Chatham area were Loyalists, who had served in the King's Regiment and Colonel Butler's Rangers. Among those who settled along the Thames were: Samuel Newkirk, Peter Shank, Nat Lewis, Thomas Williams, John Goon, William Harper, Hezekiah Wilcox, Josiah Wilcox, Hugh Holmes, John Pike, Robert Pike, Robert Simplex, Garr Brown, Thomas Clarke, Jno. Hazard, Jacob Hill and John Gordon.

Plaque commemorating Major John Richardson

Clearing the Land and the First Home

The first task of the new settlers, when they arrived at their locations, was to erect a shanty for themselves and their families. They had been supplied with canvas tents, but there were not enough to accommodate everyone, and many had to spend their first nights in the wilderness under the trees.

The men, however, shouldered the axes which the government had given them, and got together to help each other chop down a few trees and build a log cabin in the small clearing thus created. When one shanty was finished, they moved on to the next lot. Soon, everyone had at least a roof over his head. The pioneer custom of having a "bee" to share the work load remained a part of country life in Upper Canada for many years to come.

All the shanties looked alike, only their size varied according to the size of the family, but none of the houses were larger than twenty by fifteen feet. The walls were generally of round basswood logs, notched together at the corners, and piled one on top of the other to about seven or eight feet in height. The spaces between the logs were chinked with wood splinters and plastered inside and out, clay being used as the mortar. Beside the opening for the door each cabin had one window, just large enough to be fitted with four small panes of glass, each measuring 7 x 9 inches, which each family had received from the government along with a bit of putty, some nails and a few other materials for building.

As there were no boards available as yet to make doors, a blanket was hung from the inside of each cabin to keep out the wind. The roof, sloped at the back, was made of strips of elm bark or the bark of black, or swamp oak. The floor consisted of round logs split in half to provide as even a surface as could be readily obtained. Inside each cabin the hearth was laid out of flat stones and the rest of the fireplace was built of field stones and small boulders up as high as the walls. The chimney, formed of round logs, was plastered with mud.

First settlement in Upper Canada

Clearing the land

Remembering the comfortable, well-equipped homes they had left behind, these crude log shanties, bare of even a scrap of furniture, were hardly a cheerful sight to the pioneers of Upper Canada. But they were too busy to dwell on the past; they were secure at last, ready to start a new life. To the old soldier, it was no problem to construct a simple bedstead at the back of the cabin by inserting poles of suitable size between the logs that formed the walls. Benches and tables were made of split basswood, and those with carpenter skills helped the others who in turn did some of the heavy chores in exchange. It was not long before each family had their crude log cabin furnished, if not comfortably, at least with the bare necessities.

As few of the settlers possessed any worldly goods and there was nowhere to obtain anything for hundreds of miles, they all depended on the government allocation. For food, this was a three years' supply of rations consisting of flour, pork, some beef and very little salt and butter. They also received Indian blankets for coats and some coarse cloth for trousers, as well as shoes. Each was also given an axe, a spade and a hoe; two families had to share one plough and one cow; every fourth family got a whip and a cross-cut saw; and every fifth family, a set of tools consisting in part of chisels, augers, drawing-knives, pick-axes and sickles. Boats were left at convenient places along the river and the bay, for the use of the settlers. Many of the tools and implements were of inferior quality, but to the soldier accustomed to the hardships of camp life, they were god-sent and helped him to make the articles needed for domestic use.

Once their cabins were built and the most essential furniture made, the pioneers turned to the land. With their short-handled ship's axes, which had never been intended to fell large trees, they made a clearing on their land in the thick covering of forest and tangled brush, and prepared the soil to plant their grain. A few years later the settlers would begin burning the trees in the dry summer season to save some of the back-breaking labour, or they destroyed the trees by cutting all around through their bark, and when they were dead, they burned them down the following summer.

A pioneer log cabin

Early Mills

For the first few years, the settlers on the St. Lawrence and around the Bay of Quinte either ground their grain by hand as best they could, or brought it to the Kingston Mills. The people in the Royal Townships had been given a few steel hand-mills by the government, but in the Bay of Quinte area the settlers used whatever method they could devise themselves. Some made a cavity in the stump of a tree with a red-hot cannon ball to hold the grain, and fashioned a pestle or pounder from the hardest wood they could find. To have their grain ground at the mill, they had to carry it there on their backs, and tramp through the trackless woods, often for days. Others loaded their sacks on a raft or a canoe in the summer, or in the winter packed them on a hand-sleigh and drew it through the deep snow along the water's edge to the Kingston Mills, located a few miles north of the Cataraqui fort on the Cataraqui River, now the entrance to the Rideau Canal.

Erected on Governor Haldimand's instruction prior to the arrival of the Loyalists in 1782-83, the grist mill on the Cataraqui was the only one in this part of Upper Canada. As the population increased, a second mill was built in 1785, this one on the Napanee River at the site of natural falls, where the town of Napanee now stands; but it did not commence operations until early 1787. To the settlers around the Bay of Quinte, the opening of the Napanee mill was welcome news, not only because it was much closer but also because there were fewer people waiting to have their gristing done now that a second mill was working, and they could return home that much sooner.

In 1788 a grist mill was erected in Matilda Township, Dundas County, by Messrs. Coons and Shaver. It had one run of stones, and attached to it was a sawmill, sorely needed by the pioneers, who soon would want larger houses and a little more than the bare essentials to furnish them. The grist mill was capable of grinding up to a hundred bushels of wheat a day, but the sawmill did not work well and had to be abandoned. However, soon after a second mill was built in the township by John Monroe. It had three or four runs of stones as well as a gang of saws, and at the time was one of the largest mills in existence.

Early mill on the Rideau River

203

Grist and sawmills on the Napanee River
at Napanee.

An early mill on the Bay of Quinte

Other mills were erected in the late 1780's and early
1790's at Niagara Falls, at Four Mile Creek in the Niagara Peninsula, at Fort Erie, and at the Mohawk Village on the Grand
River. At Twelve Mile Creek, just below the junction of the
western and eastern arms of the creek and close to the Niagara
escarpment, a saw and grist mill were begun by Duncan
Murray in 1786. He died before the mills were completed, and
Robert Hamilton took over a year later. Another sawmill,
owned by a Mr. Street and Colonel Butler, was in operation in

the area by 1789. By 1792 there were twenty mill sites in that part of the country, located either along the Niagara River and its tributaries, on Lake Erie, or in the northern part of the peninsula.

Early mills were driven by water power, and saw and grist mills often sprang up together. Before they had a sawmill in their own neighbourhood, the settlers resorted to pit-sawing to cut boards from their timber. Using a two-handled whip-saw, one man stood in a pit below the log while another man stood on a platform on top. During the spring freshets, the rasping sound of busy saws could be heard day and night in the countryside, but when the water dwindled in the hot summer, the miller had to stop sawing to save power for the flouring mill.

The erection of a grist and sawmill was the first indication that a settlement was progressing. The mills attracted more settlers and soon became the centre around which a village was beginning to cluster. Sir John Johnson's mill, erected on the east bank of the Gananoque River and in operation by the summer of 1792, was followed three years later by Joel Stone's mill on the west bank. These two mills were the first industries at the site now occupied by the town of Gananoque. Near the mouth of the Moira River, Captain John Walden Meyers from Jessup's Loyal Rangers built a sawmill and a grist mill in the early 1790's, around which a settlement grew, known as Meyers' Creek. Later renamed Belleville, it is today a thriving city on the Bay of Quinte shore. For several years Captain Meyers' grist mill was the only one between Napanee and York (Toronto), and settlers brought their grain to his mill from as far away as Port Hope. A portion of the ancient mill is still standing today on the east bank of the Moira River.

Part of Captain Meyers' mill still standing on the Moira River, Belleville, Ontario.

C. & J. McDonald's flour and grist mill, Gananoque, built in 1826

The Hungry Years

For the first three years of settlement in Upper Canada the Loyalists' basic needs were looked after by the government, which supplied them with food rations and clothing as well as spring wheat, peas, corn and potatoes for seed. At the end of this period, the settlers were supposed to be able to stand on their own feet and provide themselves and their families with the necessities of life. Most of the settlers, by working hard and for long hours, had managed by then to clear sufficient land on which to raise the crops that would sustain them. But drought conditions and a severe winter, with four to five feet of snow on the ground until April, resulted in poor crops in 1887. This marked the beginning of a period that went down in the history of Upper Canada as the "Hungry Years". With government provisions cut off, the settlers' stores of supplies dwindled rapidly, and most families suffered severe hardships for the next two years. By the spring and summer of 1888, the mills in Kingston and Napanee had little or no grain to grind.

Hardest hit by the shortage of food were those settlers who had neglected to get their seed supplies, those who had relied entirely on the generosity of "Old George" as they called the King, and those who had no farming experience. Some settlers in the remote townships actually died of starvation during the famine that swept the country, from Quebec to the outlying settlements of Upper Canada. People who had arrived in Upper Canada too late to be entitled to government subsidies were in dire distress. They had not yet had time to cultivate any of their land, and the provisions they had been able to bring with them, on their journey through the wilderness to their new homes, were soon depleted. One farmer with a large family to feed sent his meagre savings to Quebec for flour. He received his money back, but no flour. Flour was so scarce that some people offered all they possessed, from a horse and household articles to a piece of land, in exchange for a bag of flour.

Many survived by eating roots and wild plants, or stripping the bark of certain trees to supplement their diet. A few died from eating poisonous roots. Those fortunate enough to own a cow at least had a little milk, to which they added leaves or the buds of trees. There were few farm animals to be found in Upper Canada at the time, and when a cow or an ox was accidentally killed, the bones were passed from house to house to be boiled with the wheat bran, to give it some flavour and nourishment. In the fourth township on the Bay of Quinte there was a field of early grain growing on a sunny hillside. It attracted people from miles around. As soon as the heads of the grain had grown sufficiently, they cut them off and boiled them for food. The owner of the field gladly shared his crop with others in distress. Bran boiled in a bit of water was often the only kind of meal served at the farmer's table for weeks on end. If the settlers were able to get hold of a few potatoes, they planted only the potato eye, using the rest for a meal. Children were even found digging the potato rinds out of the ground again at night, to still their hunger pangs.

Occasionally someone was able to kill a deer and add some meat to his family's diet, but most of the deer had fallen prey to hungry wolves during the long harsh winter. Pigeons and wild fowl, plentiful in Upper Canada in the early years, were strangely absent in some areas during the famine. Fish, speared by torchlight the Indian way, helped to sustain many a family, but the cry for bread continued to be heard throughout the land for some time. Settlers who were able to procure a bit of flour in Lower Canada or at Oswego willingly shared their bread with anyone who knocked at the door, even at the risk of running out of food themselves. Their common plight bonded the pioneers together, and fostered a spirit of neighbourliness; this helped them to cope during the dreadful years of the famine until relief and plenty came to most farms in the summer of 1889.

Early log house

Fishing at night

Life on the Pioneer Farm

Some of the disbanded soldiers and other Loyalist settlers had been farmers before the war. Others did not have the slightest idea what life in the country was like, let alone life as a pioneer in the wilds of Upper Canada. But most of them were hardy and determined enough, and they soon adapted to their new circumstances.

For the pioneer farmer and his family, the workday started at dawn and ended when it was time to go to sleep at night. The chores and the toil never ended. There were few comforts and even fewer luxuries the settlers could obtain in those early years, before trading posts and stores were established, or peddlers began visiting the remote areas. Left to their own resources, they made the articles they needed with their own hands, and generally found ways to cope with the problems which arose.

From the Indians the settlers learned how to prepare the fresh pelt of a deer by removing the hair and working the hide by hand with the brains of an animal until it was white and pliable enough to be made into a garment. As soon as they had cleared sufficient land, the settlers began growing flax to provide linen for their clothing. Each family sowed at least an acre of flax, and when the time came the plants were pulled up and the seeds separated from the stalks which were then exposed to the dew at night for several weeks to rot them, but without injury to the flax fibre. Then they were dried and pounded between two beams, known as a "crackle", to loosen the woody part of the stalk from the fibre. After that they were beaten or "swingled" with a piece of sword-shaped wood, and finally combed or "heckled". With rudely made implements, the women spun the grey flax fibre into threads which they could weave into a coarse linen. As soon as possible, the farmer secured a few sheep, so that their wool could be spun and turned into warm clothing for the harsh winter months. Later, spinning wheels and looms were brought to Upper Canada by some of the settlers, and eventually carding and fulling mills were established in most communities.

A new settlement grows in the backwoods of Upper Canada

211

HEWING AXES & ADZES

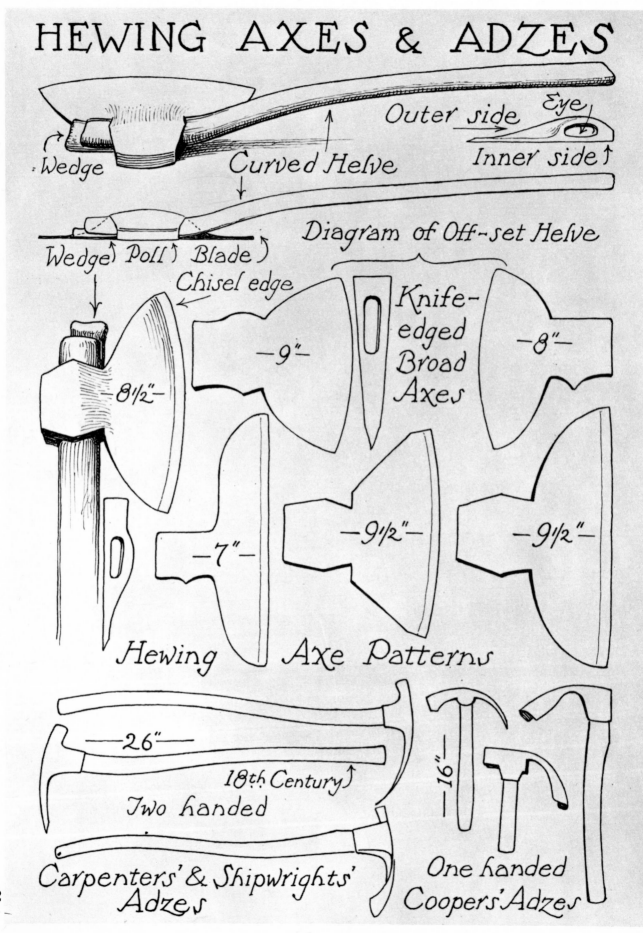

Wedge

Curved Helve

Outer side → Eye

Inner side ↑

Diagram of Off-set Helve

Wedge ↑ Poll ↑ Blade ↓

Chisel edge

Knife-edged Broad Axes

—9"—   —8"—

—8½"—

—7"—   —9½"—   —9½"—

Hewing Axe Patterns

—26"—

18th Century ↑

Two handed

—16"—

Carpenters' & Shipwrights' Adzes

One handed Coopers' Adzes

212

In the field, the farmer laboured with his own strong arms and by the sweat of his brow. For the first few years, he had no beasts of burden to help him remove the tree stumps or plough his land. Eventually oxen and a few horses could be procured from Lower Canada and from the United States, and most of the new settlers brought their own cows with them. Some of the Loyalists went back across the border to buy cattle, and drove them home through the wilderness forest with the aid of dogs. Exposed to elements and bears, some lost their way and were never seen again. In 1785 the entire livestock in the fourth township on the Bay of Quinte was comprised of a couple of horses and three cows.

Candle dipping machine

When the skins of sheep and cattle became more plentiful, each farmer quickly learned to tan the hides, dress the leather and make sorely needed shoes for himself and his family. In the evening, by the light of his hearth fire, he made a crude wooden plough, a reaping cradle, or a churn for the woman of the house to make her own butter, or a fork to add to their meagre supply of household utensils. He relied on his own ingenuity and on the advice of his neighbour. Nothing was wasted on the pioneer farm that could be utilized in some way or fashioned into some useful article. At first the women made the candles to light the house and barnyard by attaching twisted strands of cotton twine to a stick, dipping it into melted sheep or beef tallow and hanging it up to harden. The process was repeated several times a day until the candle reached the proper length. Later on, tin moulds became available, taking some of the drudgery out of the job. From wood ashes they made lye, and boiling it for a couple of hours with suet, bacon fat, or skimmings over an outdoor fire made of pine kindlings, they obtained a soft soap that could be poured into a mould to harden and was used to do the laundry. To make use of the burned timber which accrued in large quantities from the continuous land-clearing, pioneer farmers started asheries, and potash-making soon became one of the early industries in Upper Canada. Used in the manufacture of glass, soap and dyes, potash from Upper Canada was exported to other countries and provided one of the first cash incomes for the enterprising pioneer.

Orchards were planted at an early stage. Most apples were dried or stored in a barrel (made by a cooper usually found at a mill site), but a portion of the harvest was set aside to be made into cider. Although a simple process, not every farmer had the time to construct his own cider-mill, and cider-milling became another one of the early and profitable industries, for every household needed vinegar. Potatoes, turnips and carrots were stored for the winter in root cellars, built underground below the frost level. Berries and other fruits from the garden were preserved by the farm wife, who spent days on end over the hot fire in her kitchen boiling them down into jams. Butchering was one of the busiest times of the year. An experienced neighbour would always be willing to help, and usually several animals were killed in a day. The meat was cut up in pieces and salted down in a barrel. After a few weeks the hams and bacons were removed from the brine and hung up in a small log smoke-house, where a fire was kept smoldering for a week to cure the meat.

Salt and sugar were both scarce commodities in pioneer days. Imported cane sugar, when it did become available, was too expensive for most people, but thanks to the maple tree there was no shortage of sweeteners in the settlers' homes. After the first few busy years had passed, most farmers who had their own sugar bush found time each spring to make a supply of maple sugar. At first the settler followed the Indian method, but gradually, as he gained experience, he improved on the manufacturing process. As the sap was being collected from each tree early in the spring while the snow was still on the ground, it was poured into a large kettle. Over an open fire it was boiled down into a thin syrup while the fire was kept going day and night. After the syrup had been allowed to settle in a wooden vessel, it was poured back into a cauldron and fresh eggs or milk were added. The liquid was then brought to the boiling point over a slow fire, and at this stage the eggs or milk would rise to the surface carrying with them any impurities which could be skimmed off. What was left was a clear substance ready to be boiled down into actual sugar. To test the consistency of the syrup during the last boiling process, a bit was dropped onto the snow from time to time. If it hardened, it was ready to be poured into moulds and the resulting cakes of sugar were a welcome addition to the farm wife's larder.

Carding

Spinning

ROLPH, SMITH & CO

Sugar making

217

After hard work young and old gather at a country dance.

Religious Life

To the pioneer in the hostile wilderness of Upper Canada, the Bible was the greatest source of comfort. It was often the only book he had been able to bring with him. For a number of years few settlements had churches of any denomination in which to worship, or any resident ministers to preach the gospel; but most of the settlers clung to the faith of their fathers, and prayer sustained them in their daily struggle with the harsh realities of pioneer life. Devout people of different religious persuasions met at each other's houses to read the Bible and sing hymns. Far removed from civilization, and lacking religious guidance, some sought relief from hardship and loneliness in the taverns that began to spring up everywhere; drunkenness, and other vices such as "dancing and carousing", were considered to be rampant by the moralists of the day.

From the beginning the Church of England was the government-supported, or "established" church of Upper Canada, and it enjoyed as such a privileged position. Not only was the Church of England entitled to the use of income from large land holdings, known as Clergy Reserves, but its ministers prior to 1798 were the only clergymen authorized to solemnize marriages. This restriction often caused a great deal of inconvenience to couples wanting to get married, and having to travel great distances to find an authorized minister.

For the settlements along the St. Lawrence and the Bay of Quinte the closest minister for some time was the Reverend John Stuart who was the first clergyman to settle in Upper Canada. Before the Revolution he had ministered to the Mohawks at Fort Hunter, in the Mohawk Valley of New York. As a Loyalist refugee, Stuart had come to Kingston in 1785 and was appointed Chaplain to the garrison at Cataraqui. He founded the parish of St. George's in Kingston, and thus became the father of the Church of England in the province. In 1786 he opened at Kingston what was the first Grammar School in Upper Canada. Serving a large area, he founded a number of missions; he also translated the gospel into the Mohawk language.

220

C.W. JEFFERYS

The Methodist circuit rider

Another early Church of England clergyman was the Reverend John Langhorn, who settled in 1790 in Ernestown township and was instrumental in erecting a church at Bath. He visited his widely scattered flock regularly, but would perform marriage ceremonies only at his church, and only before eleven o'clock in the morning. If a couple did not arrive at the appointed time, no matter how far or how long they had travelled, he made them wait until the next morning. He always asked the groom to pay three coppers to his clerk, but would never take any money for himself. In 1797 Reverend Langhorn began to record births, marriages and deaths and continued doing so during the remaining two decades of his ministry.

The Reverend Robert Addison was sent to Upper Canada from England by the Society for Propagating the Gospel in Foreign Parts. He arrived at Niagara in 1792, and was appointed Chaplain of the Upper Canada Legislature. He also served the settlers, and became the first Rector of St. Mark's parish which was founded in 1792. St. Mark's Church, built at Newark (Niagara-on-the-Lake) between 1804 and 1809, was burned by the Americans in the War of 1812. Rebuilt some years later, it is today one of the historic landmarks of the area. Another historic Anglican church at Niagara is St. Andrew's, built in 1819, which serves a parish that erected its first log church at that place in 1794.

 Clarke, Irwin & Company Limited, Toronto, Canada.

The first Methodist church in Upper Canada at Adolphustown

St. Mark's Church, Niagara-on-the-Lake

A camp meeting

A Sunday in the backwoods of Upper Canada

223

Although the Church of England was the established church of Upper Canada, it was the Methodists with their missionary zeal who sent the first circuit-riding preachers to the scattered settlements in the province. Most of the early Methodist ministers belonged to the American Methodist Conference, and came to Canada from New York state. Many of these saddleback preachers had little education, but all were dedicated to winning souls. Dressed in black with a broad grey hat, booted and spurred, his saddle bags containing hymn book and Bible flung across his horse, he was constantly on the move, riding large circuits to preach the gospel and convert the sinners. The Methodist ministers established classes in the settlements, and appointed stewards and elders who would teach the Bible and give religious instruction after they had gone.

Among the Loyalists from New York state who settled in the St. Lawrence township of Augusta in 1785, were Paul and Barbara Heck, John Lawrence, and the family of Philip Embury. Some twenty years earlier Barbara Heck and Philip Embury had founded the Methodist Church in North America. Philip Embury died in 1775, and by the time his widow had come to Augusta she had married John Lawrence. With Barbara Heck as the driving force, the Hecks, the Lawrences, and other Methodists in the area, began holding the first Methodist classes in Upper Canada almost immediately after their arrival. Near the town of Prescott stands the small "Blue Church", built next to the graveyard where Barbara Heck was buried in 1804. A hundred years later a monument was erected at the site in her honour, and on it the inscription reads:

> Barbara Heck put her brave soul against the rugged possibilities of the future and under God, brought into existence American and Canadian Methodism, and between these her memory will ever form a most hallowed link. In memory of one who laid foundations others have built upon.

One of the early Methodist circuit riders who preached at the Hecks' house on one occasion was the Reverend William Losee. A young man, with a grave and persuasive voice, he was known to cry out in the midst of his sermon "Oh Lord, smite them!", and many a sinner felt "smitten" and repented. Losee organized the first Methodist Circuit in Canada, and its members erected in 1792 a frame meeting house on the shore of Hay Bay (Bay of Quinte) in Adolphustown township. Abandoned in 1860, this first Methodist church building was used as a granary for many years. In 1910 it was re-acquired by the Methodist Church, and today it is an historic site. It is open to visitors in the summer months, and used annually for a commemorative service by the United Church of Canada.

The first Methodist to preach in the Niagara peninsula was Major George Neale, who came to Queenston in 1786. He established a class between Queenston and St. David's at the home of Christian Warner. The first Methodist church in this district was built in 1801 and was known as Warner's Church. Darius Dunham, from the Methodist Episcopal Church of the United States, was another early preacher in the Niagara Circuit, which was formed in 1795 and extended as far as Ancaster. He went to Meyers' Creek (Belleville) that year, to conduct the first religious service in that hamlet on the Bay of Quinte.

Barbara Heck (1734-1804), the Mother of Methodism in North America. Barbara Heck and her husband settled in Augusta Township on the St. Lawrence River after the American Revolution.

St. George's Church, Kingston, 1792

In the pioneer days, the Reverend Alexander MacDonnell of Kingston, and his assistant minister, were the only two Roman Catholic priests in Upper Canada. There were not many Catholics among the early settlers, and mass was celebrated in private homes for many years. One of the first priests to be ordained by Bishop MacDonnell was the Reverend Michael Brennan, who later went to Belleville as the first parish priest.

The first Protestant church in the Canadas was established by the pioneers of Williamsburgh in Dundas County. The Lutherans of that area started building a small frame church in 1789 and invited the Reverend Samuel Schwerdfeger from Albany, New York, to become their pastor. Reverend Schwerdfeger came to Williamsburgh in the summer of 1790. As Loyalists, he and his family had suffered great hardships, having once been thrown into a dungeon for remaining steadfast to the King. Soon after his arrival at Williamsburgh, Reverend Schwerdfeger consecrated the small edifice his congregation had completed. It was known as Zion's Church.

Among the pioneer Baptist ministers of Upper Canada were Elders Wyner and Turner who, by the 1790's, served a large number of settlers of the Baptist faith in Thurlow township. There was also Elder Abel Stevens of Bastard township, who became the founder of the Baptist Church in Leeds and Grenville Counties.

The Reverend John Bethune, who had been Chaplain to the 80th Regiment during the Rebellion, came to Williamstown in Glengarry County in 1789, and was one of the first Presbyterian clergymen to minister to the settlers of Upper Canada.

A number of the Loyalists who settled at Adolphustown were Quakers. Among them were John and Philip Dorland, who were instrumental in establishing in 1798 the first organized Meeting of the Society of Friends, as the Quakers call themselves. On a corner of John Dorland's farm they erected what was the first Quaker Meeting House in Upper Canada. The congregation was known as the Adolphustown Preparative Meeting and was under the authority of New York Yearly Meeting, of which the Dorlands were members. Philip Dorland had been elected to represent the Midland District in Upper Canada's first Legislative Assembly. To discharge his duties, he rode over Indian trails to Newark (Niagara); but when he was asked to take the oath of office, he refused to do so. As a Quaker his "yea was a yea and his nay was a nay", and there was no reason to take an oath. He was willing to re-affirm his loyalty to King George III, but beyond that he would not go. Whereupon he was disqualified from taking his seat as a member of the first Parliament. He saddled his horse and rode the long way back home.

Quaker Meeting House

The Simcoe Years

On April 11, 1785 Colonel Guy Johnson and other Loyalists signed a petition to the King, asking that the country to the west of Pointe au Baudet become a district, distinct from the Province of Quebec, and that it be administered by a Lieutenant-Governor and Council with internal powers, but subordinate to the Governor of Quebec. The Loyalist settlers in the western part of what was then still the Province of Quebec, were dissatisfied with the seigneurial system of land tenure which had evolved in Quebec under French rule, and which was continued under the British government. Under this system the King was the feudal landlord renting the land to his tenants. The Loyalists wished to have the kind of tenure they had enjoyed before the war in the former British colonies, where their land had been free from seigneurial claims. Protests and petitions to that effect continued over the next few years.

In the meantime, Governor Haldimand had left for England in 1784, and after an interval of two years Guy Carleton, now Lord Dorchester, returned to Canada in 1786 to take Haldimand's place as Governor-General. On July 24, 1788, Lord Dorchester issued a proclamation dividing the western part of Quebec into four districts to be known as Lunenburgh, Mecklenburgh, Nassau and Hesse. On November 8th of that year he wrote to London, asking that "a person of fidelity and ability in the confidence of the Loyalists to superintend and lead them" should be appointed as soon as possible. Although he did not advocate a division of the province at this time, the decision to divide Quebec into Upper and Lower Canada was made soon after, and in 1791 the Canada Act (now more commonly known as the Constitutional Act) was introduced in the British Parliament to settle the details of government for the new Province of Upper Canada.

Lieutenant-Colonel John Graves Simcoe, commander of the Queen's Rangers, was appointed as the first Lieutenant-Governor of Upper Canada. He was chosen by Parliament over Sir John Johnson to the great disappointment of Lord Dorchester, who had recommended Johnson for the post.

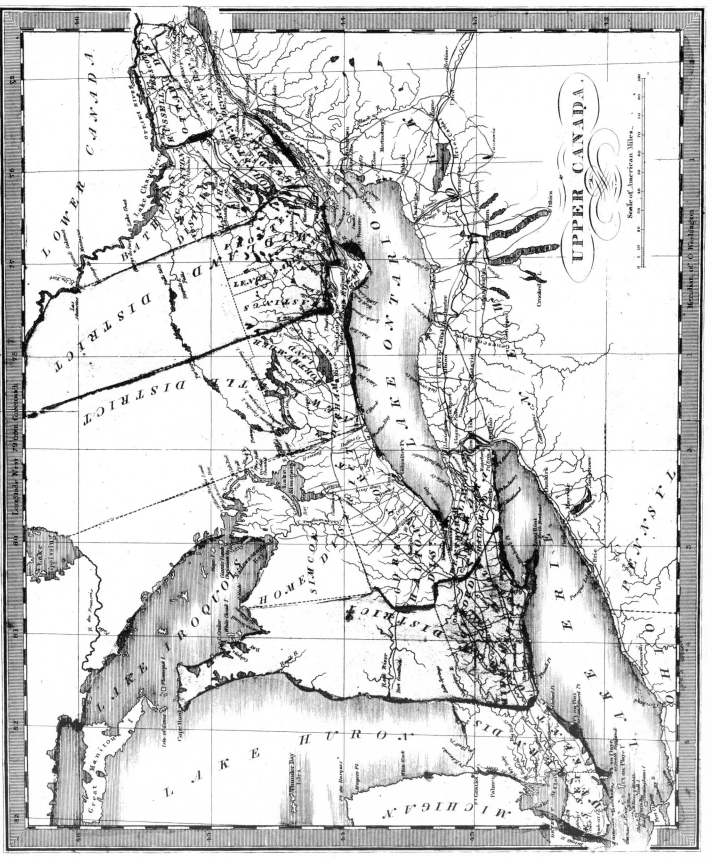

Map of the Districts of Upper Canada, 1833

229

On July 8, 1792 Simcoe took his oath of office in the small, partially-completed frame edifice of St. George's Church at Kingston, the first house of worship in that settlement. A week later, on July 16, a proclamation was read from the steps of this church, dividing the province into nineteen counties. Members of Simcoe's Executive Council present for the historic occasion were: the Hon. William Osgoode, Chief Justice; the Hon. Peter Russell, Receiver-General; and the Hon. Jacques Baby. The counties, defined in the proclamation as to their boundaries, were: Glengarry, Stormont, Dundas, Grenville, Leeds, Frontenac, Ontario, Addington, Lennox, Prince Edward, Hastings, Northumberland, Durham, York, Lincoln, Norfolk, Suffolk, Kent and Essex. The original County of Ontario then consisted of the various islands south of the mainland, between the mouth of the Gananoque River and the eastern extremity of Prince Edward County. For the time being, Upper Canada was comprised of four Districts: the Eastern District, the Midland District, the Home District, and the Western District.

Simcoe House, preserved at Upper Canada Village

On July 17, 1792, the Executive Council for Upper Canada, consisting of five members, met for the first time in a frame dwelling at the corner of Queen and King Streets at Kingston. It was here that they inaugurated representative government in the province, and chose the first Legislative Council. The first "Government House", now known as "Simcoe House", has since been moved from Kingston to Upper Canada Village to be preserved for its historical significance. Soon after his government had been established, Simcoe decided to make Newark (Niagara) his temporary capital. In 1793, however, he built a fort on the shore of Lake Ontario. It was named Fort York after the King's son, and it was to this place that Simcoe moved the permanent seat of government. Around the fort grew a settlement known as York, which is now the sprawling metropolis of Toronto and the capital of the Province of Ontario.

To ensure the progress of his vast but sparsely settled province, Simcoe, as soon as he had been designated as Lieutenant-Governor, invited new settlers. Believing that a large number of loyal subjects had remained in the States and would prefer to live again under British rule, he issued a proclamation offering free grants of the rich land in Upper Canada to all who desired to come. Lots of no more than 200 acres were to be granted to the applicants, except where the Governor approved otherwise. No individual, however, was to receive more than 1,000 acres, and all had to take an oath of allegiance promising "to maintain and defend to the utmost of my power the authority of the King in his parliament as the supreme legislature of this province". The new settlers were obliged to clear five acres of their grant, build a house, and open a road along the front of their land.

Many responded to Simcoe's call. Some came because they sincerely wished to live under British rule; others were merely attracted by the generous land grants and by the opportunities Upper Canada had to offer to anyone enterprising and willing to work. Not all the newcomers were looked upon with favour by the "old" Loyalist settlers who had known the hardships of being refugees and had fought the battles of the Revolutionary War. There were indeed some prospective settlers who entered Upper Canada, petitioned for free grants and took the oath of allegiance, only to offer their land for sale shortly thereafter and return with their profits to the States. However, the majority of settlers who came to Upper Canada from the former colonies, between the 1790's and the outbreak of the War of 1812, proved to be just as loyal to the British Crown as the earlier Loyalist settlers, upon whom the King had bestowed a title of honour in recognition of their loyalty. It was on November 9, 1789, that Lord Dorchester as the Governor-General of Canada created the Noble Order of Unity of the Empire and proclaimed the hereditary title of U.E. Loyalist to be conferred upon those who had fought for the Crown and had suffered and sacrificed so much as the King's faithful subjects. Today, the descendants of the United Empire Loyalists in Canada are friends and allies of their American neighbours to the south, but they are proud to bear the letters U.E. after their names as a mark of honour earned with the blood and tears of their pioneer ancestors.

The Armorial Bearings of the United Empire Loyalists' Association of Canada

Early Days in Upper Canada

U P P E R   C A N A D A.

GEORGE the THIRD, by the grace of GOD of Great Britain, France and Ireland king, defender of the Faith, and so forth, to all whom these presents shall come, GREETING:

KNOW ye, that WE of our special grace, certain knowledge and mere motion have given and granted, and by these presents DO GIVE and GRANT unto *Michael Gander* and *his* heirs and assigns for ever, a certain parcel or tract of land situate in the *Township of Willoughby* containing by admeasurement *One Hundred Acres* be the same more or less, being composed of lot number *Six in the second Concession* and situate, lying and being in the *Township* of *Willoughby* aforesaid, in the county of *Lincoln* and *Home* district of our province aforesaid, together with all the Woods and Waters thereon lying and being, under the reservations, limitations and conditions herein after expressed: which said *One Hundred* acres of land are butted and bounded, or may be otherwise known as follows (that is to say) *Beginning at a Post in front of the said Concession, marked S/6 then North Twenty Chains, then West Fifty Chains, then South Twenty Chains, then East Fifty Chains to the place of beginning.*

AND *whereas* by an act of the parliament of Great Britain, passed in the thirty-first year of his Majesty's reign, entitled " An act to repeal certain parts of an act passed in the fourteenth year of his Majesty's reign, entitled " An act for making more effectual provision for the government of the province of Quebec, in North America, and to make further provision for the government of the said province," it is declared, that " no grant of lands hereafter made shall be valid or effectual unless the same shall contain a specification of the lands to be allotted and appropriated solely to the maintenance of a protestant clergy within the said province:" in respect of the lands to be hereby granted, *Now know ye,* that WE have caused an allotment, or appropriation of *Fourteen Acres and two sevenths to* be made in a *certain Parallelogram in the rear of the Township of Beverly. Beginning at the South West Angle of the lands appropriated for the Clergy, for the Township of Crowland, then South 13° East, One Hundred and five Chains, then North 77° East Three Hundred and Twenty Chains, then North 13° West One Hundred and five Chains, then South 77° West Three Hundred and Twenty Chains to the place of beginning.*

being in the proportion of one to seven of the lands so hereby granted, as and for a reserve, and to and for the sole use, benefit and support of a protestant clergy being as nearly adjacent thereto as circumstances will admit, and being as nearly as circumstances and the nature of the case will admit, of the like quality as the lands in respect of which the same is allotted and appropriated, and as nearly as the same can be estimated equal in value to the seventh part of the lands so hereby granted as aforesaid. To HAVE AND TO HOLD the said parcel or tract of land to *him* the said *Michael Gander* and *his* heirs and assigns for ever, *saving* nevertheless to us, our heirs and successors all mines of gold, silver, copper, tin, lead, iron and coal that shall or may now, or hereafter be found on any part of the said parcel or tract of land hereby given and granted as aforesaid: *and saving* and reserving to us, our heirs and successors, all white pine trees that shall, or may now, or hereafter grow, or be growing on any part of the said parcel or tract of land hereby granted as aforesaid. *Provided always* that no part of the said parcel or tract of land hereby granted to the said *Michael Gander* and *his* heirs be within any of the reservations before this grant made and marked for us, our heirs and successors by our Surveyor General of Woods, or his lawful deputy, in which case this our grant for such part of the land hereby given and granted to the said *Michael Gander* heirs as aforesaid, and which upon a survey thereof being made be found within any such reservations, shall be null and void and of none effect, any thing herein contained to the contrary notwithstanding: *Provided also* that the said *Michael Gander* *his* heirs or assigns shall or do within *three* years erect and build, or cause to be erected and built in and upon some part of the said parcel or tract of land a good and sufficient dwelling house { be the said *Michael Gander* or *his* assigns not having built, or not being in his or their own right lawfully possessed of an house in our said province) and be therein, or cause some person to be therein resident for and during the space of *One year* thence next ensuing the building of the same. *Provided also* that if at any time or times hereafter the land so hereby given and granted to the said *Michael Gander* and *his* heirs, shall come into the possession and tenure of any person or persons whomsoever, either by virtue of any deed of sale, conveyance, enseoffment or exchange, or by gift, inheritance, descent, devise or marriage, such person or persons shall within twelve months next after his, her or their entry into, and possession of the same, take the oaths prescribed by law, before some one of the magistrates of our said province; and a certificate of such oaths having been so taken shall cause to be recorded in the secretary's office of the said province: IN DEFAULT of all or any of which said conditions, limitations and restrictions, this said grant, and every thing herein contained shall be, and WE do hereby declare the same to be null and void, to all intents and purposes whatsoever; and the land hereby granted, and every part and parcel thereof, shall revert to, and become vested in us, our heirs and successors in like manner as if the same had never been granted; any thing herein contained to the contrary in any wise notwithstanding.

GIVEN under the great seal of our province of Upper Canada: WITNESS *the Honorable Peter Russell President Administering the Government* of our said province, this *eighth* day of *July* in the year of our Lord one thousand *Seven Hundred & Ninety Nine* and thirty-*ninth* of our reign.

By Command of his *Honor* in Council.

Entered in the Auditors Office
17 September 1799
Peter Russell Auditor Genl

A Crown Deed

Simcoe's soldiers building road

Map of the Province of Upper Canada, 1800

The Toronto Purchase. In 1787 Lord Dorchester met with the Chiefs of the Mississauga Indians to purchase the land at the foot of what is now Dufferin Street, Toronto, and the land north on either side of a trail to Lake Simcoe. Settlement at Toronto, known in the early days as York, did not begin until 1793, when it was chosen as the seat of government for Upper Canada.

Crown Land Seal—1801.

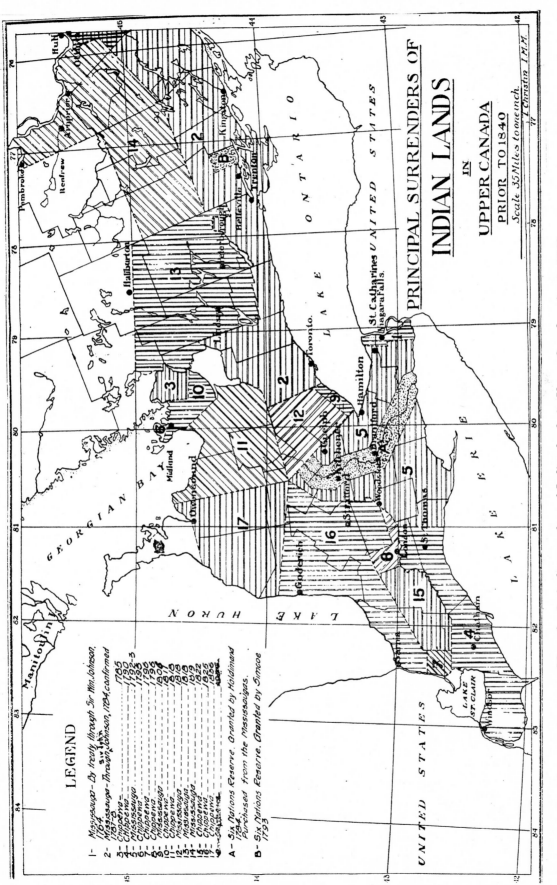

Map of principal surrenders of Indian lands in Upper Canada prior to 1840.

A view of Cataraqui at the entrance of Lake Ontario, taken from Captain Brant's house, July 16, 1784, by James Peachey.

Corduroy roads, built in swampy areas, were named after the long-wearing ridged cloth in common use.

Early schoolhouse

Clearing the land. The pioneer farmer with his yoke of oxen removes
a stump before seeding the land.

Ferry operated by horse

The first St. Lawrence Canal, 1781

Weller's Stage Line from York to Kingston

An early trading post

At Fort York, Toronto

Stone Blockhouse in
Fort Wellington, Prescott, Ont

At
Kingston Mills to
guard Rideau Canal

Blockhouses in Upper Canada

Old blockhouse at Kingston

243

The first homestead in Upper Canada

The old Adolphustown church, Upper Canada's first Methodist Church. This view was taken June 22, 1892, at the centennial gathering.

Group of United Empire Loyalists at the monument in Adolphustown.

An historical plaque commemorating the Loyalists in Upper Canada was unveiled adjacent to the Legislature Chambers in the main Parliament Building at Queen's Park, Toronto, on May 27, 1967, by the Dominion President Mr. E. J. Chard.

The plaque bears the following inscription:

THE LOYALISTS IN UPPER CANADA

When the United Empire Loyalists who had "adhered to the Crown" during the American Revolution and, in most cases, served in volunteer regiments, came to settle in this Province in the 1780's, the region was largely uninhabited. These Loyalists, all of whom had suffered persecution and confiscation of property, were granted land in the vicinity of the Bay of Quinte and the Upper St. Lawrence, Niagara and Detroit Rivers. They laid the foundation of a new province. It was largely because of their presence that a form of self-government, based on British law and institutions, was established in Upper Canada when the province was created in 1791. By then the Loyalists numbered about 10,000.

Bibliography

Abbott, W. C., *New York in the American Revolution*, New York, 1929

Adams, C. F., *The Works of John Adams*, Vol. 2, Boston, Massachusetts, 1856

Adams, C. F., *Familiar Letters of John Adams*, New York, 1876

Adams, James T., *Revolutionary New England*, Vol. 2, New York, 1968

Adams, Randolph, *Political Ideas of the American Revolution*, N.Y., 1958

Alden, John R., *The South in the Revolution, 1763-1789*, Baton Rouge, 1957

Alden, John R., *History of the American Revolution 1775-1783*, New York, 1954

Allan, Herbert, *John Hancock, Patriot in Purple*, New York, 1948

Allen, Gardner W., *A Naval History of the American Revolution*, Williamstown, 1970

American Historical Review, IV, January 1889 No. 2

Anburey, Thomas, *With Burgoyne from Quebec*, 1789

Andrews, Charles M., *The Colonial Background of the American Revolution*, New Haven, 1924

Arnold, Isaac. *The Life of Benedict Arnold*, Chicago, 1880

Ashe, Samuel A., *History of North Carolina*, Greensboro, 1908

Bailyn, Bernard, *The Ideological Origins of the American Revolution*, Cambridge, 1967

Baldwin, Alice, *The New England Clergy and the American Revolution*, New York, 1965

Barker, Charles A., *The Background of the Revolution in Maryland*, New Haven, 1967

Barnes, Donald G., *George III and William Pitt, 1783-1806*, Stanford, 1936

Bancroft, George, *History of the United States*, New York

Barck, Oscar T., *New York City During the War for Independence*, New York, 1931

Bates, Walter, *Kingston and the Loyalists of 1783*, St. John, N.B., 1889

Baxter, J. P., *The British Invasion from the North*, Albany, 1887

Boucher, Jonathan, *Reminiscences of Maryland Loyalist*, London, 1909

Brinton, Crane, *The Anatomy of Revolution*, New York, 1960

Brown, J. B., *View of Canada and the Colonists*, 1844

Bruce, R. M., *The Loyalist Trail*

Burgoyne, John, *A State of the Expedition from Canada*, London, 1780

Burke, Edmund, *Speech on American Taxation*, London, 1775

Burt, Alfred L., *The Old Province of Quebec*, Minneapolis, 1933

Butterfield, L. H., *The Diary and Autobiography of John Adams*, Cambridge, 1962

Callahan, North, *Royal Raiders, The Tories of the American Revolution*, New York, 1963

Campbell, William W., *Annals of Tryon County*, New York, 1831

Canniff, William, *History of the Settlement of Upper Canada*, 1869

Carnochan, J., *History of Niagara*, 1914

Carrington, H. B., *Battles of the American Revolution*, New York, 1876

Carter, J. S., *The Story of Dundas County*, 1905

Catton, Bruce, *The American Revolution*, New York, 1971

Chitwood, Oliver P., *A History of Colonial America*, N.Y., 1961

Clarke, Charles, *Sixty Years in Upper Canada*, 1908

Collection of the Massachusetts Historical Society, Boston, 1852-71, Fourth Series

Collection of the New York Historical Society for the Year 1880, New York, 1881

Colburn, H. Trevor, *The Colonial Experience*, Boston, Massachusetts, 1966

Coffin, V., *The Province of Quebec and the Early American Revolution*, Madison, 1896

Coleman, Kenneth, *American Revolution in Georgia*, Athens, 1958

Conant, Thomas, *Upper Canada Sketches*, 1898

Conant, Thomas, *Life in Canada*, 1903

Corwin, Edward S., *French Policy and the American Alliance of 1778*, Princeton, 1916

Coupland, Reginald, *The Quebec Act, A Study in Statesmanship*, Oxford, England, 1925

Coupland, Reginald, *The American Revolution and the British Empire*, New York, 1930

Crary, Catherine S., *The Price of Loyalty*, New York, 1973

Croil, James, *Dundas County*, 1861

Cruikshank, E. A., *Some Papers of An Early Settler*, 1890-1

Cruikshank, E. A., *The Story of Butler's Rangers*, Welland, 1893

Cumberland, Barlow, *Canoe, Sail and Steam*

Cushing, H. A., *The Writings of Samuel Adams*, Vol. 3, New York, 1907

Davidson, Philip, *Propaganda and the American Revolution*, Chapel Hill, 1941

Dickerson, O. M., *The Navigation Act and the American Revolution*, Philadelphia, 1951

Dorson, Richard M., *America Rebels*, New York, 1953

Dupuy, R. E. T., *The Compact History of the Revolutionary War*, New York, 1963

Einstein, Lewis, *Divided Loyalists*, London, 1933

Evans, G. N. D., *Allegiance in America, The Case of the Loyalists*, London, 1969

Fisher, Sydney G., *The Struggle for American Independence*, Philadelphia, 1908

Fisher, Sydney G., *The True History of the American Revolution*, Philadelphia, 1902

Flick, Alexander C., *Loyalism in New York During the American Revolution*, New York, 1901

Fraser, Alexander, *A History of Ontario*, 1907

Gipson, Lawrence, *The Coming of the Revolution, 1763-1775*, New York, 1954

Goodwin, A., *The American and French Revolutions 1763-93*, Cambridge, 1965

Gourlay, J. L., *History of the Ottawa Valley*, 1896

Gourlay, Robert, *A Statistical Account of Upper Canada*, 3 volumes, 1822

Guedalla, Philip, *Fathers of the Revolution*, New York, 1926

Haight, Canniff, *Country Life in Canada 50 Years Ago*, 1885

Hancock, Harold B., *The Delaware Loyalists*, Wilmington, 1940

Harrell, I. S., *Loyalism in Virginia*, Durham, N.C., 1926

Harrington, Virginia D., *The New York Merchants on the Eve of the Revolution*, N.Y., 1935

Hawke, David, *Colonial History, Reading and Documents*, New York, 1966

Henry, George, *The Emigrant's Guide*

Heriot, George, *History of Canada*, 1804

Heriot, George, *Travel Through the Canadas*, 1807

Herrington, W. S., *The History of Lennox and Addington*, 1913

Herrington, W. S., *Pioneer Life Among the Loyalists of Upper Canada*, 1915

Hilbreth, Richard, *History of the United States of America*, New York, 1849

Hudleston, Francis J., *Gentleman Johnny Burgoyne*, Wilmington, 1940

Hoffman, Robert V., *The Revolutionary Scene in New Jersey*, New York, 1942

Hulton, Ann, *Letters of a Loyalist Lady*, Cambridge, 1927

Jackson, H. M., *Roger's Rangers*, 1953

Jackson, John N., *St. Catharines, Its Early Years*, Belleville, 1976

Jenson, Merrill, *The Founding of a Nation*, New York, 1968

Jones, E. Alfred, *The Loyalists of Massachusetts*, London, 1930

Jones, Thomas, *History of New York During the Revolutionary War*, N.Y., 1879

Ketchum, Richard, *The American Heritage Book of the Revolution*, New York, 1958

Kirby, William, *Annals of Niagara*, Lundy's Lane, 1896

Kirby, William, *The United Empire Loyalist of Canada*, 1884

Knollenberg, Bernhard, *Origin of the American Revolution 1759-1766* N.Y., 1960

Labaree, Leonard W., *Conservatism in Early American History*, Ithaca, 1959

Lajeunesse, Ernest, *The Windsor Border Region*, Toronto, 1960

Langton, John, *Early Days in Upper Canada; Letters of John Langton*, 1926

Lapp, Eula C., *To Their Heirs Forever*, Picton, 1970

Lossing, Benson, *War of Independence*, New York, 1847

MacLean, J. P., *Flora MacDonald in America*, Lumberton, N.C., 1905

Miller, John C., *Origin of the American Revolution*, Boston, 1943

Miller, John C., *Sam Adams: Pioneer in Propaganda*, Stanford, 1936

Moore, Frank, *Diary of the American Revolution*, N.Y., 1860

Morgan, Edmund S., *The Birth of the Republic, 1763-1789*, Chicago, 1956

Morison, Samuel E., *Oxford History of the American People*, N.Y., 1965

Morris, Richard B., *The American Revolution A Brief History*, N.Y., 1955

Nelson, William, *The American Tory*, London, 1961

Newcomer, Lee M., *The Embattled Farmers*, N.Y., 1953

Nickerson, Hoffman, *The Turning Point of the Revolution*, Boston, 1928

Paterson, G. G., *Land Settlement in Upper Canada 1783-1840*, Ont. Archives, 1920

Peck, Epaphroditus, *The Loyalists of Connecticut*, New Haven, 1934

Playter, George, *History of Methodism in Canada*, 1862

Reaman, G. E., *The Trail of the Black Walnut*, Toronto, 1957

Sabine L., *Loyalists of the American Revolution*, Boston, 1864, 2 vols.

Schlesinger, Arthur M., *Colonial Merchants and the American Revolution, 1763-1776*, N.Y., 1939

Siebert, Wilbur, *The Flight of American Loyalists to the British Isles*, Columbus, 1911

Siebert, W. H., *The Loyalists of Pennsylvania*, 1929

Smith, Justin H., *Our Struggle for The Fourteenth Colony*, N.Y., 1907

Stanley, George F. G., *Canada Invaded*, Toronto, 1973

Stark, James H., *Loyalists of Massachusetts*, Boston, 1910

Swiggett, Howard, *War out of Niagara*, New York, 1933

Trevelyan, Sir George Otto, *The American Revolution*, London, 1921

Upton, L. F. S., *The United Empire Loyalists: Men and Myths*, Toronto, 1967

Van Tyne, C. H., *The Loyalists in the American Revolution*, N.Y., 1959

Van Tyne, C. H., *The Causes of the War of Independence*, New York, 1922

Wahlke, John C., *The Causes of the American Revolution*, Boston, 1962

Wallace Stewart, *The United Empire Loyalists*, Toronto, 1922

Wilcox, William B., *Sir Henry Clinton, the American Rebellion*, New Haven, 1954

Wilson, James G., *The Memorial History of the City of New York*, New York, 1892

List of Illustrations
and
Acknowledgements

For the illustrations and related material assembled in this book we are most grateful to the Public Archives of Canada; Douglas Library, Queen's University, Kingston; United Empire Loyalists' Association of Canada; and the historical societies, libraries, museums and private persons, whose names appear below.

Page 8) Map of Canada 1809, *Douglas Library, Queen's University*; 10) His Majesty George William Frederick the Third, *The Public Archives of Canada*; 11) Briton Behold the Best of Kings, *courtesy, American Antiquarian Society*; 12) (top) William Pitt, *The Pictorial Field-Book of the Revolution, Lossing*; (left) Map showing location of Fort Duquesne, *Douglas Library, Queen's University*; (right) George Augustus, Lord Howe, reprinted from *Montcalm at the Battle of Carillon by Maurice Sautai*; 13) James Murray, *Mika Collection*;

14) View of Montreal. 1760, reprinted from *The Fall of New France*; View of Quebec City, *Mika Collection*; 15) A map of the British Empire in North America, *Douglas Library, Queen's University*; 16) John Hancock, *The Pictorial Field-Book of the Revolution, Lossing*; 17) James Otis, *The Pictorial Field-Book of the Revolution, Lossing*; Private, Tenth Regiment of Foot, *The Public Archives of Canada*; 18) George Grenville, *The Pictorial Field-Book of Revolution, Lossing*; 19) (top) Edmund Burke, *The Pictorial Field-Book of Revolution, Lossing*; The Stamp Act, reprinted from *The Loyalists of Massachusetts, J. Stark*; 20) (top left) Stamps, *Mika Collection*; (top right) Demonstration, *War of Independence, Lossing*; Pennsylvania Journal, reprinted from *Pictorial Field-Book of Revolution, Lossing*; 21) (top) Burning stamps, *Library of Congress*; Funeral of the Act, *The John Carter Brown Library*; 24) John Adams, *Mika Collection*; The Coroner's inquest, *The Bostonian Society*; 25) The Boston Massacre, *The Metropolitan Museum of Art, Gift of Mrs. Russell Sage, 1910*; 26-27) Description of "Boston Massacre", *Boston Gazette*; 29) "The Boston Tea Party", *courtesy, National Archives, Washington*; 30) "Society of Patriotic Ladies", *Library of Congress*; 31) View of Boston, 1768, *by Paul Revere*; 33) "Quebec Act", *The Public Archives of Canada*; 34) The Political boundaries of Quebec, reprinted from *St. Catharines, Ontario, John N. Jackson*; 35) View of Quebec, 1760, reprinted from *The Face of New France*;

36) Samuel Adams, *The Pictorial Field-Book of Revolution, Lossing*; 38) Bostonians Paying the Exciseman, from *The Loyalists of Massachusetts, J. Stark*; 39) The Tory's Day of Judgement, *Library of Congress*; 41) Carpenter's Hall, reprinted from *The Story the Revolution, H. C. Lodge*; 42) City and Port of Philadelphia, *The Stranger in America*; 43) Treasury Note, *The Pictorial Field-Book of Revolution, Lossing*;

45) Persecution of Loyalist, *Mika Collection*; 47) Sons of Liberty, *Historical Society of Pennsylvania*; 48) Thomas Gage, *Mika Collection*; 49) Loyalists' exodus, *Mika Collection*; 50) Patrick Henry, *The American Revolution, Chase*; 51) Unite or Die, *The Pictorial Field-Book of Revolution, Lossing*; A New Song, reprinted from *The True History of the American Revolution, Fisher*; 52) "America", *British Museum*; 53) Lord North, *The Pictorial Field-Book of Revolution, Lossing*; Confrontation at Lexington, *The Pictorial Field-Book of Revolution, Lossing*; 54) Battle of Lexington, *The Pictorial Field-Book of Revolution, Lossing*; Retreat from Concord, *The Pictorial Field-Book of Revolution, Lossing*; 55) Paul Revere, *The American Revolution, Chase*; Boston besieged, *The Pictorial Field-Book of Revolution, Lossing*; 56) Patriot Ethan Allen, *The True History of the American Revolution, Fisher*; Fort Ticonderoga, reprinted from *Our Struggle for the Fourteenth Colony, Smith*; 57) "Olive Branch Petition", *New York Public Library*; The State House in Philadelphia, reprinted from *The Story of the Revolution, H. C. Lodge*; 58) General George Washington, *Mika Collection*; 59) The Battle of Bunker Hill, *The Pictorial Field-Book of Revolution, Lossing*; View of Boston, *The Pictorial Field-Book of Revolution, Lossing*; 60) A Royal Welsh Fusilier reprinted from *History of the Royal Welsh Fusiliers, Cannon*; and American Rifle Man, *Anne S. K. Brown Collection*; 61) Sir William Howe, *New York Public Library*; 62) Evacuation of Boston, *Mika Collection*;

63) General Richard Montgomery, *The Pictorial Field-Book of Revolution, Lossing*; 65) Governor Carleton on Place D'Armes, *Mika Collection*; March of Benedict Arnold, *The Pictorial Field-Book of Revolution, Lossing*; 66) March of Benedict Arnold, *The Public Archives of Canada*; 67) Sir Guy Carleton, *The Public Archives of Canada*; A view of St. Johns, *The Pictorial Field-Book of Revolution, Lossing*; 68) General Montgomery attacks Quebec, *Mika Collection*; Benedict Arnold's Headquarters, *Canadian Illustrated News*; 69) General Montgomery wounded, *The Public Archives of Canada*; 70) Johnson Hall, *John B. Knox, Lake Pleasant, N.Y.*; The Highland Company, *The Public Archives of Canada*; 71) Sir William Johnson, *Mika Collection*; 71) Colonel Guy Johnson, *New York Historical Association, Cooperstown, N.Y.*; Sir John Johnson, reprinted from *Stormont, Dundas and Glengarry, Harkness*; 73) Joseph Brant, *Mika Collection*; 74) British and French soldiers, *The Public Archives of Canada*; 75) Street in Albany, *Mika Collection*; View of Fort Johnson, *Mika Collection*; 76) Scottish soldiers, *Tartans by Ch. Hesketh*; Flora MacDonald, *Library of Congress*;

78) A Proclamation, *The Story of the Revolution, H. C. Lodge*; 79) Thomas Jefferson, *American Revolution, Cullen*; 80) First draft of the Declaration of

Independence, *Library of Congress*; Benjamin Franklin, *The Public Archives of Canada*; 81) Declaration of Independence, *New York Journal*; 83) Andrew Oliver, *The Loyalists of Massachusetts, J. Stark*; 84) The Patriotic Barber, *Library of Congress*; 85) Trapped Loyalist, *New York Public Library*; 87) Newgate, *The Connecticut Historical Society*; 88) John Malcolm, *John Carter Brown Library*; Toppling the statue of King George III, *Mika Collection*; Continental paper money, *The Pictorial Field-Book of Revolution, Lossing*; 89) William Franklin is arrested, *The Loyalists of Massachusetts, J. Stark*; New York *by Faden, 1776*; 90) General Sir William Howe, *courtesy of William L. Clements Library, University of Michigan*; 91) Map of Hudson River, *Mika Collection*; 92) Burning of the city of New York, *Library of Congress*; General Washington, *National Archives*; 93) Admiral Lord Howe, *Library of Congress*; British troops landing at New York, *British Museum*; 95) General Frederick Riedesel, *Mika Collection*, View of the Hudson River, *With Burgoyne from Quebec*; 96) View of Fort Edward, *B. J. Lossing*; 98) General Burgoyne addressing Indians, *The Public Archives of Canada*; 99) General Burgoyne, *The Public Archives of Canada*; 100) German Dragoon, *Mika Collection*, Bennington Monument, *Mika Collection*; The Battle of Bennington, *The Pictorial Field-Book of Revolution, Lossing*; 101) The Bennington battlefield, *Mika Collection*; Plaques on the Bennington battlefield, *Mika Collection*; The Headpiece of the Grenadier's Uniform, 1776, *Cannon*; 102) Colonel Barry St. Leger, *Mika Collection*; General Horatio Gates, *The Pictorial Field-Book of Revolution, Lossing*; 105) Gates' Acceptance of Surrender, *With Burgoyne from Quebec*; 106) General Buroyne surrenders, *Mika Collection*; Encampment of the Convention Army, *Douglas Library, Queen's University*; 108) Colonel John Simcoe, *Metropolitan Toronto Central Library*;

109) A Queen's Ranger, *The Public Archives of Canada*; 110) Colonel Banastre Tarleton, *New York Public Library*; 111) The King's Proclamation, reprinted from *An American History, Muzzey*; A British private, *The Public Archives of Canada*; 112) The Wyoming Valley Massacre, *Chicago Historical Society*; 113) The Queen's Rangers, *The Public Archives of Canada*; 114) Articles of Military Equipment, *The Public Archives of Canada*; 115) Appeal for volunteers, *New York Public Library*; Cartoon accusing General Howe, *New York Historical Society*; The Controversy, *Douglas Library, Queen's University*; 118) Sir Frederick Haldimand, from *Sir Frederick Haldimand, McIlwraith*; 120) View of Sorel, *The Pictorial Field-Book of Revolution, Lossing*; A blockhouse and sawmill, *Douglas Library, Queen's University*; Blockhouses, (left) *Douglas Library, Queen's University*, (right) *The Public Archives of Canada*; 122) Routes of Loyalists, *Mika Collection*; 123) Loyalists travelling, *The Public Archives of Canada*; 124) Loyalists camping, *The Public Archives of Canada*; 126) Lord Cornwallis, *The United Empire Loyalists, Wallace*; 127) Surrender of Cornwallis, *The Pictorial Field-Book of Revolution, Lossing*; British cannon, *Mika Collection*; 128) View of the "Surrender Field" and Monument, *Mika Collection*; 129) Map of the siege of Yorktown, *Douglas Library, Queen's*

University; 130) Sir Henry Clinton, *Kean Archives*; 131) Map of the Acadian Peninsula, *The Acadian Exiles by A. G. Doughty*; 132) American Loyalists, *The Pictorial Field-Book of Revolution, Lossing*; 133) Major Samuel Holland, *The Public Archives of Canada*; Sir John Johnson, *Metropolitan Toronto Library*; 135) Fort Cataraqui, *Kingston Whig-Standard*; Map of Loyalists' settlement, *Mika Collection*; 137) A view of the Fort Cataraqui, *The Public Archives of Canada*; 138) View of the St. Lawrence, *Ontario Archives, Toronto*; 139) The St. Lawrence River, *Ontario Archives, Toronto*; 141) Map of the Detroit River, *Archives du Ministere des Colonies, Paris*; Fort Niagara, reprinted from *History of Niagara, Carnochan*; 142) Chief Joseph Brant, *The Public Archives of Canada*; 143) A view of Niagara, *Niagara Historical Society*; 144) Major Robert Rogers, *The Public Archives of Canada*; Ranger, *Lossing*; 146) Uniform of British regular, *The Public Archives of Canada*; 147) Durham boats, reprinted from *Upper Canada Sketches, Conant*; 149) Camp in the forest, *The Public Archives of Canada*; 150) The Mohawk Indians, *oil painting by Rev. Bowen Squire*;

152) Settlers drawing location tickets, *The Public Archives of Canada*; 155) Encampment of Loyalists, *The Public Archives of Canada*; 156) Plaque at Williamstown, *Mika Collection*; 157) Settlers building log cabin, *British North America*; 158) Thousand Islands, *Ontario Archives, Toronto*; 159) Logging scene, reprinted from *Upper Canada Sketches, Conant*; 161) Brockville Court House, *Canadian Illustrated News*; 162) Map of Royal Townships, *The Public Archives of Canada*; 163) Joel Stone, *The Public Archives of Canada*; A plaque honouring Joel Stone, *Ontario Dept. Travel and Publicity*; 164) A plaque honouring William Buell, *Ontario Dept. Travel and Publicity*; A plaque honouring William Merrick, *Ontario Dept. Travel and Publicity*; 166) Reverend John Stuart, *The Public Archives of Canada*; 167) Loyalists landing at Adolphustown, *oil painting by Rev. Bowen Squire*; 168) St. John's Church, *Lennox and Addington County Historical Society's Museum*; 169) The White House, *Ontario Dept. Travel and Publicity*; 170) Church of *St. Alban-the-Martyr, Mika Collection*; 171) The Loyalist landing place, *Mika Collection*; Loyalist Monument, *Mika Collection*; 172) Site at Adolphustown, *Mika Collection*; Memorial to U. E. Loyalists, *Ontario Dept. Travel and Publicity*; 173) Map of Cataraqui Townships, *The Public Archives of Canada*; 174) Marysburgh Settlement, *Mika Collection*; 175) The Rose House, *Mika Collection*; 176) The White Chapel, *Mika Collection*; 177) First settlement, reprinted from *Upper Canada Sketches, Conant*; 178) Loyalist monument, *Mika Collection*; 179) Maple sugar making, *Canadian Illustrated News*; 181) Mill on the Apannee River, *Lennox and Addington County Historical Society's Museum*; 182) Bush Road, *Public Archives of Canada*; 183) Bush Farm, *Public Archives of Canada*; 185) Indians, *British North America*; 186) Indian hunter, *The Public Archives of Canada*; 187) Colonel John Butler, *Ontario Archives, Toronto*; 188) A Butler's Ranger, *Howard Swiggett*; Butler's Burying Ground; *John Burtniak Collection*; 189) Map of the Western Settlement, *The Public Archives of Canada*; 191) Thomas

Merritt, *St. Catharines Public Library;* 192) Potash making, reprinted from *Upper Canada Sketches, Conant;* 193) The Nelles Manor, *Ontario Dept. Travel and Publicity;* 194) Plaque commemorating Samuel Ryerse, *Ontario Dept. Travel and Publicity;* 196) Map of Detroit River, *The Public Archives of Canada;* 197) Plaque commemorating Major John Richardson, *Mika Collection;* 199) First settlement, *The Public Archives of Canada;* 200) Clearing the land. *painting by Rev. Bowen Squire;* 201) A pioneer log cabin, *The Public Archives of Canada;* 203) Early mill, *William Henry Bartlett;* 204) Grist and sawmill, *Lennox and Addington County Historical Society's Museum;* An early mill, *painting by Rev. Bowen Squire;* 205) Capt. Meyers' mill, *Mika Collection;* 206) Mill at Gananoque, *The Public Archives of Canada;* 208) Early log house, *J. N. Jackson;* 209) Fishing at night, reprinted from *Country Life in Canada, Haight;* 211) A new settlement, *Canadian Illustrated News;* 212) Hewing — Axes and Adzes, *The Public Archives of Canada;* 213) Candle dipping machine, *The Public Archives of Canada;* 215) Spinning and carding, *The Public Archives of Canada;* 216) Spinning, reprinted from *Country Life in Canada, Haight;* 217) Sugar making. reprinted from *Country Life in Canada, Haight;* 218) Country Dance, *The Public Archives of Canada;* 220) The Methodist rider, *The Public Archives of Canada;* 221) Church in Adolphustown, *copyright The Book Society of Canada Limited, reprinted by permission of the publisher;* 222) St. Mark's Church, *Canadian Illustrated News;* A camp meeting, reprinted from *Upper Canada Sketches, Conant;* 223) A Sunday in the backwoods, *Canadian Illustrated News;* 225) Barbara Heck, *John Street United Methodist Church;* 226) St. George's Church, *Douglas Library, Queen's University;* 227) Quaker Meeting House, reprinted from *Country Life in Canada;* 229) Map of Upper Canada 1833, *Douglas Library, Queen's University;* 230) Simcoe House, *Douglas Library, Queen's University;* 232) Coat of Arms, U. E. L., *The United Empire Loyalists' Association of Canada;* 233) A Crown Deed, *Lennox and Addington County Historical Society's Museum;* 234) Building road, *The Public Archives of Canada;* 235) Map of Upper Canada, *Douglas Library, Queen's University;* 236) The Toronto Purchase, *from the Confederation Gallery of Canadian History;* Crown Land Seal, *Ontario Archives, Toronto;* 237) Indians' Lands, *Ontario Archives, Toronto;* 238) A view of Cataraqui, *The Public Archives of Canada;* 239) Corduroy Roads, *painting by Rev. Bowen Squire;* Early schoolhouse, *Lennox and Addington County Historical Society's Museum;* 240) Clearing the Land, *painting by Rev. Bowen Squire;* Ferry operated by horse, *painting by O. C. Madden, Napanee;* 241) The first St. Lawrence Canal, *The Public Archives of Canada;* Weller's Stage, *courtesy of Toronto Public Library;* 242) An early trading post, *The Public Archives of Canada;* 243) Blockhouses in Upper Canada, *The Public Archives of Canada;* Old blockhouse at Kingston, *Mika Collection;* 244) The first homestead, reprinted from *Country Life in Canada, Haight;* The old Adolphustown church, *Lennox and Addington County Historical Society's Museum;* 245) United Empire Loyalists, *Lennox and Addington County Historical Society's Museum;* Plaque commemorating the Loyalists in Upper Canada, *Ontario Dept. Travel and Publicity.*

Index

251